**GILLIAN CLEMENTS** was born and brought up in Sussex, and
studied Illustration under Raymond Briggs at Brighton Polytechnic.
She is an armchair explorer who did a degree in Geography at
Newcastle University. She has a fascination with world history and
was inspired to write this book by her desire to discover exciting facts
about different parts of the world. Gillian's first book for
Frances Lincoln was *The Picture History of Great Inventors*.
She lives in Hereford, England.

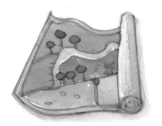

# THE PICTURE HISTORY
## of
# GREAT
# EXPLORERS

**Gillian Clements**

**FRANCES LINCOLN CHILDREN'S BOOKS**

# CONTENTS

"I don't pretend to understand the Universe –
it's a good deal bigger than I am..."

*Thomas Carlyle (1795–1881)*

# INTRODUCTION

Like any other animal, the very first humans – of East and South Africa – toiled hard to live off the land. Their constant search for food and water made explorers of them all. Thousands of generations on, human ingenuity and adaptability have made it possible for us to live in almost every landscape and climate in the world.

The 15th century was the beginning of the 'Great Age of European Exploration'. With skilful navigation and good maps, famous captains like Christopher Columbus, Vasco da Gama and James Cook set sail across the oceans and began to span the globe. These adventurers and their crews must have been brave, even heroic men. However, all too often their voyages, fired by curiosity, religious fervour and hopes of profit from trade, led to slavery, disease and death for the people they met, whose lands they claimed for Europe.

We are one world. When you see the Earth from space, this is very clear. The new frontiers for today's explorers are the Moon and Mars. Let's hope that this time we won't destroy what we find. Perhaps alien space explorers will discover *us* first. What will happen then?

*Gillian Clements*

# The First Explorers

Modern scientists disagree about who our human ancestors are. Some experts believe that we are descended from Australopithicenes, a tribe of ape-like humanoids who lived in South and East Africa between four and one million years ago. Others believe that we evolved from another, completely different branch of the ape family, and that one day fossils will be found to prove it.

In the Ice Age, lower sea levels helped create a land bridge between Asia and North America, across the Bering Sea. Today's Inuits are descendants of the first humans who crossed from Asia, around 24,000 BC.

Siberian land bridge

Inuit

N. AMERICA

Atlantic Ocean

North American Indian

Native Americans in North, Middle and South America are also descended from Asians who crossed the Bering Strait. After the crossing they split into many different tribal groups.

S. AMERICA

South American Indian

What we can be sure of is that in the last two million years or so, some of our ancient ancestors left Africa and looked for new places to settle. They began to use better tools, hunt more efficiently, and work with fire. Over time, they spread all over the world.

## OUR EXPLORER-ANCESTORS MIGRATED THROUGHOUT THE WORLD.

c5,000,000 years ago
Fossils suggest that Australopithicenes exist in South Africa.

c2,000,000 years ago
The most recent Ice Age begins.

c1,700,000 years ago
Homo erectus lives in East Africa.

c250,000 BC
Ancient Homo sapiens appears in East Africa.

**Australopithecus** 'Southern Ape' c5-1,000,000 years ago

**Homo habilis** 'Handy Man' c1,8-1,200,000 years ago

**Homo erectus** 'Upright Man' c1,500,000 years ago

**Homo sapiens** 'Wise man' c400,000-250,000 BC

**Neanderthal Man** c130,000 BC

**Homo sapiens sapiens** Modern humans c100,00 BC

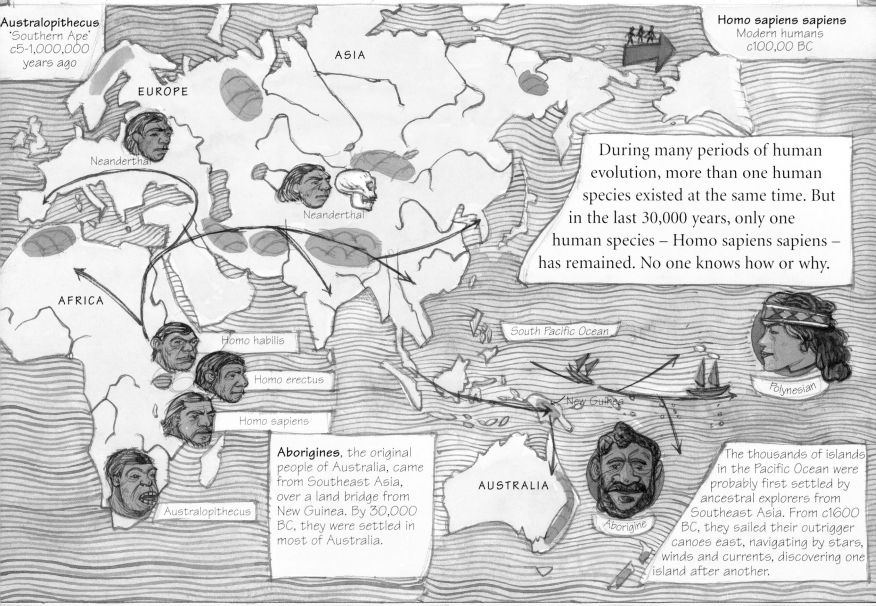

ASIA

EUROPE

Neanderthal

Neanderthal

AFRICA

Homo habilis

Homo erectus

Homo sapiens

Australopithecus

South Pacific Ocean

New Guinea

Polynesian

AUSTRALIA

Aborigine

During many periods of human evolution, more than one human species existed at the same time. But in the last 30,000 years, only one human species – Homo sapiens sapiens – has remained. No one knows how or why.

**Aborigines**, the original people of Australia, came from Southeast Asia, over a land bridge from New Guinea. By 30,000 BC, they were settled in most of Australia.

The thousands of islands in the Pacific Ocean were probably first settled by ancestral explorers from Southeast Asia. From c1600 BC, they sailed their outrigger canoes east, navigating by stars, winds and currents, discovering one island after another.

# TODAY'S HUMAN RACES ALL BELONG TO ONE SPECIES: HOMO SAPIENS SAPIENS.

**c200,000 BC**
Neanderthal Man lives in Europe and Asia.

**c150,000 BC**
Modern Homo sapiens sapiens migrates to Europe and Australia.

**c35,000 BC**
Neanderthals become extinct in Europe.

# The Ancient Explorers

**Herkouf c2420 BC**
The Egyptian prince Herkouf used donkeys and slaves to carry ivory, precious stones, ebony and frankincense from Nubia up the Nile Valley.

**Hanno 5th century BC**
The Carthaginian Hanno took 60 ships along the West African coast, and may have got as far as the Bight of Benin.

The period in history we refer to as the 'Ancient World' began when people started to write. As conquerors and traders, the explorers of this time travelled far and wide. In ancient Egypt, traders sailed papyrus boats carrying gems and spices. Two thousand years later, the Phoenician merchants of the Mediterranean travelled to West Africa. By 400 BC, the ancient Greeks had reached Britain and Asia; the Chinese were trading with the Arabs; and Polynesians were crossing the South Pacific, seeking island homes.

**Alexander the Great 356-323 BC**
In his short life, Alexander marched his army through lands from Persia to Egypt, defeating kingdoms, and founding cities like Alexandria.

**Hatsepsut 1480 BC**
Hoping they would find precious myrrh, this female Egyptian ruler ordered five ships to the Land of Punt (probably in today's Somalia).

**Herodotus 5th century BC**
This Greek explored Egypt, Athens, Italy and the Black Sea, studying their history and making accurate maps.

**Himlico c450 BC**
This Carthaginian sailed beyond the Mediterranean, past the Spanish and French coasts, to buy tin from Ireland and 'Tin Land' (Britain).

## THE ANCIENT EXPLORERS SOUGHT KNOWLEDGE, TRADE AND CONQUEST.

**c2,500 BC** Egypt sends its first expedition to Nubia in the south.

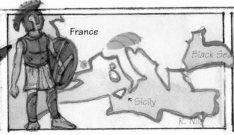

**734-600 BC** The Greeks set up colonies in Sicily, on the Black Sea, on the Nile and in France.

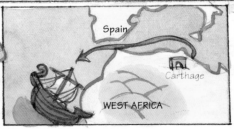

**c470 BC** Carthaginians explore the West African coast.

**327 BC** Alexander crosses the Hindu Kush mountains to invade NW India.

**Polybius c168 BC**
Polybius the Greek explored the Roman Empire, travelling through Asia Minor, Egypt, Italy, France and Spain. His *Universal History* was made up of 40 volumes.

**Chang-Ch'ien c130 BC**
Chang-Ch'ien explored Central Asia, and founded the Silk Road, which linked Chinese traders with merchants from India and the Middle East – even Persia and Rome.

ASIA

Pacific Ocean

Silk Road

Syria

ASIA MINOR

Iraq

Indus R.

ARABIA

Pakistan

CHINA

INDIA

Arab trade route

**Julius Caesar c55 BC**
This ambitious Roman Emperor visited, and conquered, most of Central Europe. He travelled to Gaul (France) and Britain on his campaigns to win more lands for Rome.

**Ptolemy 90-168 AD**
Ptolemy was a Greek geographer, astronomer and mathematician – and a great explorer.

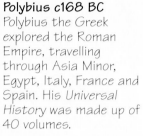

# PTOLEMY'S *GEOGRAPHY* CONTAINED EVERYTHING EUROPE KNEW ABOUT THE WORLD.

AFRICA

**204 BC** Roman general Scipio Africanus Major invades Africa.

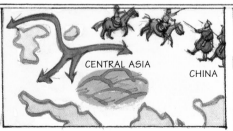

CENTRAL ASIA

CHINA

**91 BC** Hun tribes defeat China's army in Central Asia.

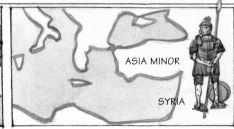

ASIA MINOR

SYRIA

**66 BC** Romans conquer territory in Asia Minor and Syria.

ASIA

**c50 BC** Romans trade with India for Chinese silk and spices.

# c484  Saint Brendan  c577

Labrador  Iceland
Faeroe Islands
Newfoundland
Ireland
North Atlantic

If the fantastical story of Saint Brendan the Voyager is true, the first Europeans to set foot in America were Irish monks, way back in the sixth century. Saint Brendan and his crew sailed west from Ireland in a curragh (a small leather boat), and were gone for seven years. On his return home, Saint Brendan remembered the islands they had seen.

He described 'giant sheep' on some – perhaps he meant the long-haired sheep that graze on the Faeroes. On other islands, which may have been the Shetlands, the monks heard birds singing in Latin. One island boasted a fiery mountain – could this have been one of Iceland's volcanoes? After stopping to pray on the back of a 'sleeping whale' (so Saint Brendan wrote), the monks steered the curragh past a group of silvery columns – were these actually icebergs drifting south off Labrador and Newfoundland?

The monks eventually reached a place they called the 'Land of Saints', which some people believe was the North American mainland. Centuries later, Christopher Columbus read Saint Brendan's colourful tale. Maybe the monk was the inspiration for his own amazing voyage to America.

In 1976 Tim Severin sailed a replica curragh, which he called Brendan, from Iceland to Newfoundland. It was proof that Saint Brendan's original voyage was possible.

Saint Brendan became the patron saint of sailors, mariners, boatmen, travellers... and whales!

*In dulce jubilo!*

## ON A QUEST FOR A 'LAND OF PROMISE', BRENDAN MAY HAVE DISCOVERED AMERIC

c400-600 Fierce Barbarians cross Europe to attack the Roman Empire.

500 Polynesians sail across the Pacific and make a new home on Easter Island.

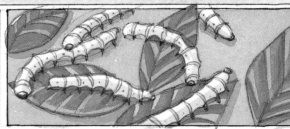

561 Christian missionaries smuggle silkworms from China to the Byzantine court.

# c970  Leif Eriksson  c1020

GREENLAND

ICELAND

NORWAY

If Saint Brendan and his companions did not reach Newfoundland, perhaps Leif Eriksson was the first European to reach North America. When he and 35 fellow Vikings drifted west of Greenland in AD 1000, they landed on the southern tip of Baffin Island, which is now part of Canada. The landscape was wild and rocky so the Vikings named it 'Helluland', which means 'land of stone slabs'. Sailing south, the explorers came across a wooded island. They named it 'Markland', which means 'land of woods'. Again they sailed south, to Nova Scotia, or maybe Cape Cod. The country was lush and fertile, and overgrown with blueberry bushes. The Vikings mistook the blueberries for grapes and named the island 'Vinland' ('wine land'). But this plentiful land was too far from home. When spring came, Leif and his men loaded their boat with timber and blueberries, and sailed back to Greenland.

Baffin Island
• 'Helluland'

Newfoundland
'Markland' •

• Nova Scotia
'Vinland'

In 1960, archaeologists uncovered the remains of Viking houses and artefacts at L'Anse aux Meadows in Newfoundland. This is proof that Leif Eriksson could have been there.

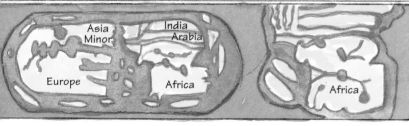

## Other Great Viking Explorers:

**Erik the Red**

Leif's father, Erik, discovered Greenland while exiled from Iceland. He set up a colony with his wife, but it died out mysteriously 500 years later.

**Bjarni Herjolfsson**

Bjarni sighted America 15 years before his friend Leif, but lost his bearings and decided not to drop anchor.

**Thorvald and Thorstein**

Leif's brothers Thorvald and Thorstein both made journeys to Vinland, with fatal consequences – Thorvald was killed by Indians and Thorstein died from sickness.

**Thorfinn Karselfni**

Thorstein's widow married Thorfinn. Their son, born in 1004, was the first European to be born in America (Vinland).

**Freydis**

On a visit to Vinland around 1020, Lief's half-sister Freydis arranged for two of her companions to be murdered. The story goes that she also killed their wives – with an axe!

## OFFICIALLY, LEIF ERIKSSON WAS THE FIRST EUROPEAN TO REACH AMERICA.

Asia Minor

Europe

India Arabia

Africa

Africa

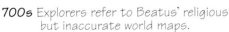

**700s** Explorers refer to Beatus' religious but inaccurate world maps.

**868** Vikings use primitive compasses made from magnetic lodestone to navigate between Norway and Iceland.

# c1216 Kublai Khan 1294

Like his grandfather before him – the great Genghis Khan – Emperor Kublai Khan had boundless energy and vision. Under his fearless command, the Mongol army advanced into new territories, crushed opposing forces, and completed the conquest of China. The huge Mongol Empire eventually stretched all the way from the Pacific Ocean in the east to Hungary in the west. North to south it spanned the Arctic coast of Asia right down to Turkey and the Persian Gulf.

China under the Mongols was probably the wealthiest, most civilized part of the medieval world. Kublai ruled from a beautiful gilded palace in Cambulac (now Beijing). Visitors to the palace were greeted at the nearby port of Kinsai, which was crisscrossed with magnificent canals.

But Kublai was careful not to let his power affect his judgement. He was a thoughtful and well-travelled ruler, who welcomed outsiders and encouraged trade. He allowed Christians from the West to travel along the ancient trade routes linking Europe and Asia, and traders from the Middle East to sail into China's ports in junks or dhows laden with Indian spices.

## FROM HIS MONGOLIAN HOMELAND KUBLAI KHAN TRAVELLED SOUTH TO CONQUER CHIN

**1086** Earliest written reference to a magnetic navigating compass (in an essay by Chinese scientist Shen Kua).

**1155** The first printed map is made – of west China.

**1200s** Chinese junks sail as far as Africa.

**1200s** Stern rudders are introduced to aid steering.

14

# c1254 Marco Polo 1324

Marco Polo's father and uncle were the first Europeans ever to cross the Asian continent to Cathay (China). By the time they set out on their next adventure, in 1271, Marco Polo was old enough to accompany them. The men journeyed for three years, until they reached the magnificent summer palace of Xanadu. The great Kublai Khan was there to welcome them, and took Marco Polo into his service at once. Marco travelled the Mongol Empire for nearly twenty years as the emperor's diplomat. He learnt four languages and much about Chinese customs.

Not long after Marco returned home to Venice, he was captured by the city's rivals, the Genoese. He used his time in prison to make a record of his amazing journey. *The Book of Marvels* is a description of China's wonders: the postal system, good roads, hot water on tap, paper money, even a burning black stone – coal. But some people thought Marco Polo was telling stories. They found it difficult to believe in dog-headed men and magicians who could control the weather. On his deathbed, the old explorer only commented, "I did not write half of what I saw."

*I did not write half of what I saw.*

**OLO'S VIVID DESCRIPTIONS OF CHINA FIRED THE IMAGINATION OF EUROPEAN TRADERS.**

**1245** John of Pian del Carpini, an elderly Franciscan monk, takes a message of peace from the Pope to the Mongol Court.

**1253** William of Rubruck is sent by the French king Louis IX to the Mongol emperor to win some influence for France.

**1291** John of Montecorvino sails from Italy to India and China, and converts many people to the Catholic faith.

All the monks hoped to find Prester John, who was believed to be a Christian ruler in the East and therefore a powerful ally. Sadly, he did not exist.

# 1304 Ibn Battuta 1368

Mecca

Ibn Battuta narrowly escaped a beheading, bandits, and even a sinking ship during his travels. He didn't write much about his private life, but we know he married four times and was father to many children.

The great Moroccan traveller Ibn Battuta began his journeys in 1325, after his first hajj (pilgrimage to the holy city of Mecca in Saudi Arabia). In thirty years he covered 120,000 kilometres – always returning to Mecca, but rarely by the same route. His first journey took him across the Arabian Desert to today's Iran and Iraq. Then he sailed beyond the equator to Zanzibar in East Africa. He embarked on his third, and most ambitious journey in 1330. After a sea voyage to Turkey, he travelled through southern Russia, Afghanistan, and across central Asia. He finally reached India in 1333 and, over the next 12 years, travelled to Sri Lanka, Chittagong (Bangladesh) and Sumatra. It was on his return from an exploratory mission in China, in 1349, that he learned that his mother back in Morocco had died of the Black Death (Bubonic plague). He decided to make two final journeys – to Muslim Spain and to the African kingdom of Mali. Back home, he wrote down his tale in a scholarly handbook, or Rihla, along with notes on the Islamic faith.

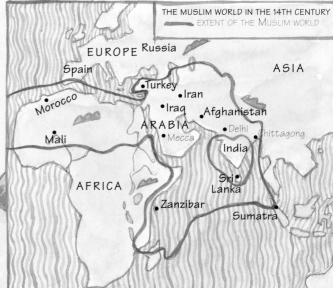

THE MUSLIM WORLD IN THE 14TH CENTURY
EXTENT OF THE MUSLIM WORLD

EUROPE Russia
Spain
ASIA
Morocco
Turkey
Iran
Iraq
Afghanistan
ARABIA
Delhi
Chittagong
Mali
Mecca
India
AFRICA
Sri Lanka
Zanzibar
Sumatra

## IBN BATTUTA'S JOURNEYS TOOK HIM ALL OVER THE ISLAMIC WORLD.

**1300s** The pivot, or dry compass is widely used in Chinese navigation.

**1325** The Aztecs build the city of Tenochtitlán on a lake in Mexico.

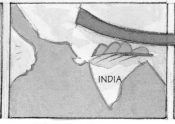

INDIA

**1332** The first cases of Bubonic plague are reported in India.

China

**1341-3** The plague breaks out in China.

**1347** Rat fleas carry the Black Death to Europe, where it wipes out 75 million.

The Pope's Order of Christ paid for many of Henry's expeditions, and all the sails on Henry's ships bore its sign – a large red cross.

Just like their European rivals, the Portuguese in the 14th century wanted more than anything to plant their flag along Africa's west coast, get rich from African gold, and set up profitable trade links. Their eventual success in doing all these things loosened the Muslim hold on many parts of the world at that time.

The European 'Golden Age of Discovery', as it has become known, was set into motion by Henry, a Portuguese prince. As the Governor of Ceuta in Morocco, he paid sea captains to explore and claim new territories for Portugal. One of his early crews reached the Madeira Islands west of Morocco. Later, at his Portuguese court in Sagres, Henry assembled a group of seamen, mapmakers, astronomers, instrument makers and ship builders, and set them off in search of a southerly trade route to India.

Unhappily for them, they had to pass Cape Bojador first, where people believed monsters lurked and the sea was so hot it boiled. It wasn't until Henry's brave captain, Gil Eanes, took his terrified crew past the Cape in 1434 that the spell was broken. Other captains followed, and went on to Senegal and the Gambia River. Not long before Henry died, one of his captains discovered the Cape Verde Islands.

Portugal · Spain · *caravel*

Sagres

Morocco

Cape Bojador

AFRICA

Senegal

Gambia River

## THE PORTUGUESE SECURED TRADE ROUTES AND BUILT UP THEIR CHRISTIAN EMPIRE.

**1400s** The Portuguese cross the seas in caravels with sophisticated triangular and square sails.

**1433** Chinese ships reach East Africa.

**1437** Brilliant Islamic astronomers make accurate observations of the stars and planets.

**1440** The invention of printing in Europe aids exploration and learning.

# 1450 Bartolomeu Dias 1500

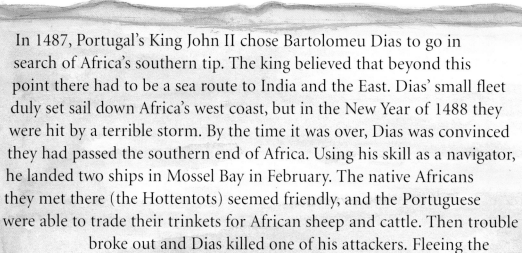

In 1487, Portugal's King John II chose Bartolomeu Dias to go in search of Africa's southern tip. The king believed that beyond this point there had to be a sea route to India and the East. Dias' small fleet duly set sail down Africa's west coast, but in the New Year of 1488 they were hit by a terrible storm. By the time it was over, Dias was convinced they had passed the southern end of Africa. Using his skill as a navigator, he landed two ships in Mossel Bay in February. The native Africans they met there (the Hottentots) seemed friendly, and the Portuguese were able to trade their trinkets for African sheep and cattle. Then trouble broke out and Dias killed one of his attackers. Fleeing the scene, he and his men headed East past a bay (now Port Elizabeth), and a river (probably the Great Fish River). Finally, weary with exploring, they turned round and headed home. As Dias steered, he looked on Africa's majestic southern cape and named it the 'Cape of Storms'.

Back in Portugal, the King thought 'Cape of Good Hope' would be a luckier name than Dias' 'Cape of Storms'. But it wasn't lucky for Dias: in 1500 a storm struck his ship off the Cape, and he drowned.

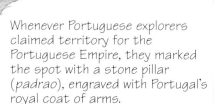

Whenever Portuguese explorers claimed territory for the Portuguese Empire, they marked the spot with a stone pillar (*padrao*), engraved with Portugal's royal coat of arms.

*Map labels: Portugal, Lisbon, Atlantic Ocean, AFRICA, South Atlantic Ocean, Walvis Bay*

DETAILED MAP OF SOUTH AFRICA

*Map labels: Cape of Good Hope, Port Elizabeth, Mossel Bay, Algo Bay*

## DIAS PROVED THAT IT WOULD BE POSSIBLE TO SAIL FROM EUROPE TO INDIA.

**1480** Leonardo da Vinci designs a parachute.

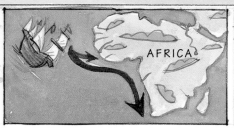

**1480s** Portuguese explorers start trading with Africa.

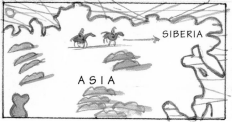

**1483** The Russians begin to explore Siberia.

**1488** Portugal's King John II refuses to fund Columbus' voyage west.

18

# 1450 John Cabot 1498

The young Italian, Giovanni Caboto, longed to travel beyond the Mediterranean to Asia, land of spices and Chinese silks. He couldn't believe his luck when some wealthy merchants and England's King Henry VII agreed to finance a voyage. Like Columbus, John Cabot (as he now called himself) believed the best way to reach the East was by sailing west across the Atlantic. He set out in the small ship *Matthew* in May 1497 from Bristol, England's busy western port. When he and his 18 crewmen reached North America 35 days later, they believed that their 'New Found Land' was Asia. They didn't find any silks and spices, but reported instead on waters teeming with fish, a fertile land and a warm climate. Cabot sailed west again the following year. This time he took a crew of 200 in five ships. One ship had to return to England for repairs. The other four, and Cabot, were never heard of again.

After his 1497 voyage, people called Cabot 'The Grand Admiral'. Interestingly, his family name, 'Caboto', literally means 'coastal sailor'.

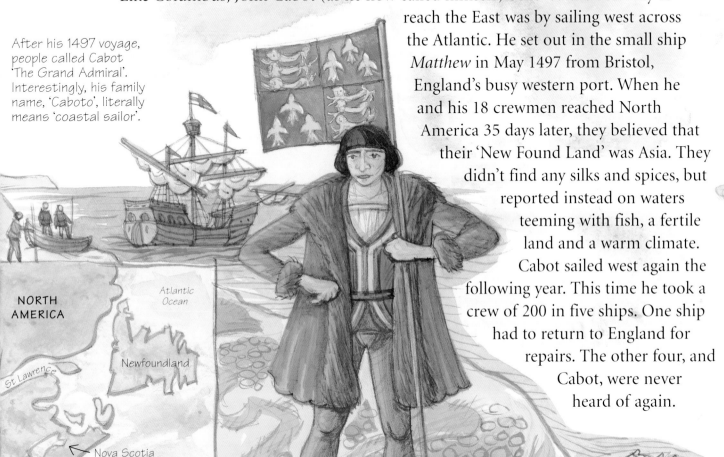

John Cabot's son Sebastian also explored and made maps. Searching for a route to Asia in 1509, he sailed to North America for the King of England, and then to South America for Spain in 1526.

As an old man, Sebastian advised the English Merchant Adventurers Company about a northeast route to Asia.

The spices most highly prized by European traders were pepper, nutmeg, cloves and cinnamon.

## JOHN CABOT SAILED WEST IN SEARCH OF EASTERN SPICE.

**1492** Book printing and publishing helps news travel fast in Europe.

**1494** The New World is divided between Spain and Portugal under the Treaty of Tordesillas.

# 1451 Christopher Columbus 1506

Columbus was an Italian cloth merchant, who first began sailing on trading voyages with his father. As he got older, he read Marco Polo's accounts of his travels in the East, and was inspired to become an explorer himself. He had a theory, based on Marco Polo's wild miscalculations, that the eastern side of Asia was much closer to Western Europe than most geographers of the time believed. In fact, during his ten years of exploring, Columbus proved just the opposite: that the world was far larger than anyone had ever imagined, with vast uncharted lands and seas. If Columbus had known how far away Asia really was, or how wide the Atlantic Ocean was, he never would have set out. As it was, he made an incredible discovery – America – and changed the course of history for ever.

Columbus studied the ideas of Ptolemy, the ancient Greek astronomer. Ptolemy's ideas led Columbus to believe the Earth was much smaller than it really is.

What Europeans didn't know about the rest of the world, they made up. Some mapmakers imagined Africans with six arms, or faces where their chests should be!

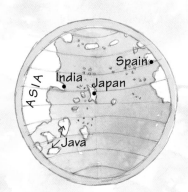

Like everyone else at the time, the mapmakers of the 15th century didn't know North and South America existed.

Columbus calculated latitude using a quadrant, or cross-staff. His pilot 'logged' the ship's speed with a plank, and the direction with a compass and traverse board. His 'dead reckoning' position was then marked on a sheepskin chart.

## COLUMBUS SAILED WEST ACROSS THE ATLANTIC, EXPECTING TO REACH THE EAST.

**1492** Martin Behaim makes the first globe, in Nuremberg, Germany.

**1492** The Catholic Spanish bring more land under Spanish control by defeating Granada, a Muslim kingdom inside Spain.

**1495** In his *Garden of Earthly Delights*, Bosch imagines the monsters that lurk outside the known world.

NORTH AMERICA

SPAIN

Atlantic Ocean

Cuba

Hispaniola

Jamaica

CENTRAL AMERICA

SOUTH AMERICA

Panama

Orinoco River

AFRICA

Navidad • • Isabella

Santa Domingo

HISPANIOLA

All of Columbus' voyages were paid for by King Ferdinand and Queen Isabella of Spain. When he set sail in 1492 across the Atlantic towards India, he was under orders from them to find gold and to claim any land discovered on behalf of the Spanish kingdom. He left port at dawn on 3 August with 90 men and three ships – the *Niña*, the *Pinta* and the *Santa Maria*. The wild Atlantic terrified the crews and at one point they threatened to throw Columbus overboard. Everyone was relieved when the *Santa Maria* eventually reached Hispaniola (Haiti) on 5 December – which they mistakenly believed was Japan. They were met by Native Americans on the shore.

On his third voyage, in 1498, Columbus landed near the Orinoco River on the mainland of South America. He made charts of "a great land, unknown till now". However, his final voyage in 1502 ended badly, and Columbus returned to Spain a bitter man. Although the old navigator had grown rich from his travels, people thought he had been cruel to the Native Americans, and this made him unpopular. King Ferdinand and Queen Isabella accused him of blackening the name of Spain because he had forced thousands of the natives into slavery. Worse still, Columbus' ships and crews had brought terrible diseases from Europe. As a result, most of the population around these islands was wiped out, all within fifty years of the explorer's first historic voyage.

Native Americans in Hispaniola

*Pinta*

*Niña*

*Santa Maria*

The *Pinta* and the *Niña* were fast caravels. Columbus' *Santa Maria* was a nao, a clumsy cargo ship.

## HE FOUND AMERICA INSTEAD, BUT DIED BELIEVING IT WAS ASIA.

**1495** Columbus sends 500 Native American women to Spain as slaves.

**1496** Romano Pane, a monk on Columbus' voyage, discovers the tobacco plant.

**1505** Searching for a sea route to India, Portuguese explorers reach East Africa.

# c1460 Vasco da Gama 1524

The Portuguese Vasco da Gama was the first European to reach India by sea. The discovery of this sea route was very important because it enabled Portugal to control all trade between Europe and India from then on. Da Gama left port in July 1497, headed down the west coast of Africa with four ships and a tough crew of 170. After rounding the Cape, his fleet soon sailed beyond the point Bartolomeu Dias had reached a decade before, and Da Gama named Natal on Africa's east coast. It was a difficult journey: Da Gama and his Christian crew were a threat to the Muslim traders in the region, and trouble broke out in every port. In Malindi, Da Gama finally convinced a local pilot to guide the ships across the Indian Ocean. He reached Calicut on India's west coast on 21 May, 1498. The Hindu ruler in Calicut declared himself insulted by the European's offerings of gold, silver, coral and scarlet cloth, but agreed to trade a few precious stones and spices. Only 55 of Da Gama's crew survived the voyage home; the rest died of scurvy.

Admiral Vasco da Gama's arms, given to him by King Manuel I after Da Gama's first voyage to India.

Scurvy is caused by a lack of vitamin C. It rotted the men's gums, which oozed black blood. The same thing happened to their legs. The sailors cut open the worst areas to let out the blood, and then rubbed and rinsed the wounds with urine.

## DA GAMA'S FAMOUS VOYAGE BROUGHT PORTUGAL TRADE AND POWER.

c1490 The Incas expand their empire in South America.

1492 Leonardo da Vinci designs a flying machine.

1495 Portugal, like Spain, expels its Jewish population.

# 1451 Amerigo Vespucci 1512

Vespucci was a 'Renaissance Man', which means he was modern and educated. He understood astronomy, cosmography and geography, and was an excellent mathematician. He also loved poetry and could read Latin.

In 1499, the merchant-navigator Amerigo Vespucci joined a Spanish expedition sailing west in search of India. They reached South America at today's Guiana and, like so many seafarers before them, believed the land they had arrived at was East Asia. Vespucci alone wasn't so sure. As the fleet sailed south to the mouth of the Amazon, and later searched the Caribbean for slaves and pearls, he busied himself studying sea currents and southern constellations. On a later expedition, for the Portuguese this time, Vespucci returned to South America. Hugging the coastline to Patagonia, he named Rio de Janeiro and the River Plate. He observed the local people, wrote notes about the animals and plants, and continued studying his maps and the stars. Finally, he concluded that the land they were seeing was not East Asia at all, but an entirely different, separate continent! The German geographer Waldseemüller named the continent 'America' in recognition of Amerigo's important discovery.

One young man went ashore from Vespucci's ship to speak to some Patagonian Indians. Unfortunately, they hacked the poor man to pieces and roasted him. When he was cooked, they ate him.

**REALISING IT WASN'T ASIA, AMERIGO VESPUCCI REVEALED A 'NEW WORLD'.**

**1500** Cabral accidentally reaches Brazil, claiming it for Portugal.

**1500** Da Vinci designs a helicopter.

**1502** In Central America, Montezuma II becomes the Aztec king.

**1507** Waldseemüller makes a map of Vespucci's 'New World', which he names 'America'.

# 1485 Hernán Cortés 1547

The Spaniard Hernán Cortés sunk all his money into an expedition to the kingdom of the Aztecs (today's Mexico) in 1519. Officially, his aim was to win territory for Spain's growing Catholic empire, but he also expected a handsome return from his personal investment, in the form of Aztec gold. Despite only a tiny force – 11 ships, 16 horses, 600 soldiers and 100 sailors – he quickly overcame defenders along the Mexican coast. Then he and his men headed inland, spreading the word of Christianity amongst the Indians and gathering volunteers to help them fight against the Aztecs. They founded the village of Veracruz ('True Cross') as a statement of their newly won power. When they eventually reached the Aztec capital of Tenochtitlán, the Spaniards ransacked the city for gold and took the emperor, Montezuma, prisoner. Few survived the terrible bloodshed that followed. But it was the diseases that the Europeans brought which put the seal on the Spanish victory. The Aztecs had no defence against smallpox, and the city fell to Spain within eighty days.

Quetzalcoatl – the principal Aztec god – was believed to have white skin and a black beard, and was expected to return to Mexico from the east. So when Cortés and his army arrived, the emperor wasn't sure if they were men or gods.

The Aztecs believed that they had to 'feed' their gods with human sacrifices, or the sun wouldn't rise. They imprisoned their enemies, like the Tlaxcalans, and killed up to 50,000 of them a year at Tenochtitlán's great temple.

The Aztecs had never seen horses. They mistook the Spaniards on horseback for fantastical beasts with two heads and six legs.

Lake Texcoco
Tenochtitlán
Tlaxcala
Veracruz
Atlantic Ocean
MEXICO

## CORTÉS CONQUERED THE AZTEC EMPIRE AND TOOK THE LAND FOR SPAIN.

**1516** Indigo dye reaches Europe.

**1517** Coffee reaches Europe.

**1520s** Chinese porcelain reaches Europe.

**1520** Chocolate made from the Mexican cocoa plant reaches Spain.

**1521** Chinese silk-making methods reach France.

**1524** South American turkeys reach England.

# 1476 Francisco Pizarro 1541

Like Cortés, Pizarro was a ruthless conquistador, greedy for New World gold. He began his career early in the 16th century, crossing Panama and sighting the Pacific Ocean with fellow countryman Balboa. Both men grew rich from their travels, but Pizarro had heard stories about the fabulous wealth of Peru's Inca Empire. In pursuit of South American gold, he set off on a risky expedition south in 1524.

When Pizarro fell out with Diego de Almagro, he arranged for his brothers – the 'viper's brood', as they were known – to murder him. But Almagro was avenged when his own son killed Pizarro.

Balboa, who discovered an overland route across Panama to the Pacific, was beheaded in 1519 on a false treason charge brought by Pizarro.

On reaching the town of Tumbes, Pizarro and his companion – Diego de Almagro – realised they were going to need reinforcements if they were to mount a successful attack. The king of Spain finally came to their aid and, in 1531, they led 180 men and 27 horses from their camp at San Miguel against the Inca kingdom. Fortunately for them, the Inca people were already weakened by European diseases and civil war, and were easily defeated.

Pizarro arrived in Cajamarca to confront Atahualpa, the 13th and last Inca emperor, in August of the following year. The emperor refused to bow to Spain, or convert to its faith, so the Spaniards murdered his guards and took him prisoner. They later killed him, despite a ransom of enough gold and silver to fill a room. Pizarro went on to take the Inca capital, Cuzco, and in 1535, to found Lima – the City of Kings.

Panama

ic Ocean
• Tumbes
• San Miguel
• Cajamarca
• Lima     PERU

Atlantic Ocean

## PIZARRO'S LUST FOR GOLD DESTROYED THE MAGNIFICENT INCA EMPIRE.

smallpox

**1530s** European and African diseases kill thousands of Incas.

**1533** The German, Frisius, develops triangulation, a new method of surveying.

**1535** Swedish archbishop Olaus Magnus commissions his own map of the world.

**1537** Flemish mapmaker Mercator uses the names America and North America on his maps.

# 1480  Ferdinand Magellan  1521

With a fleet of five ships and about 250 men, the Portuguese explorer Ferdinand Magellan set off on his historic voyage around the world in September 1519, from southern Spain. His intention at the time was to find a western route to the Spice Islands. All went according to plan until the fleet reached South America, where trouble broke out amongst the men and Magellan executed two of his captains. Magellan eventually led a reduced fleet of three ships through the choppy waters of the 'Magellan Strait' in the autumn of 1520. Incredibly, this strait took them through the islands near the southern tip of South America, all the way out to the calm, open sea. Magellan named the ocean the 'Pacific'. But he had no idea of the terrible four-month crossing that lay ahead. Crazed and almost starved, his dwindled crew landed in the Philippines in April 1521, where Magellan himself was killed by angry Mactan islanders. Only 18 of the original crew were left alive when the fleet arrived back in Spain. These ill and desperate men had completed the first ever circumnavigation of the world by sea.

Magellan's Spanish captains disliked him, probably because he was Portuguese.

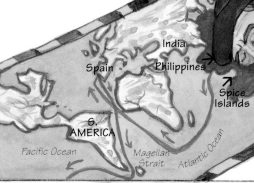

Magellan proved the Earth was round, but underestimated its size. Instead of crossing the Pacific to the Spice Islands in a few days, it took nearly four months.

The Spaniard Juan Sebastian del Cano took command after Magellan was killed. He completed Magellan's circumnavigation of the world.

To keep themselves alive while they sailed across the Pacific, the crew drank foul, yellow water, and ate rat-nibbled biscuits, sawdust soup, ox-hide from the rigging, and rats.

India
Philippines
Spain
Spice Islands
S. AMERICA
Pacific Ocean
Magellan Strait
Atlantic Ocean

## MAGELLAN WAS THE FIRST TO FIND A SEA ROUTE ALL THE WAY AROUND THE WORLD.

**1512** Copernicus declares that the Earth (and other planets) orbits the Sun.

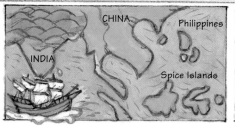

CHINA
Philippines
INDIA
Spice Islands

**1510s-20s** The Portuguese set up trading posts in the Spice Islands, China and Ceylon.

Hudson R.
New York

**1524** Verrazano finds New York Bay and the Hudson River.

N. AMERICA
West Coast
S. AMERICA

**1529** Diego Ribero's maps of America include the Pacific West Coast.

# 1491  Jacques Cartier  1557

Cartier originally sailed from France looking for a route to Asia, but he is remembered today for his exploration of Canada. He embarked on his first voyage in 1534, headed west. Sailing along Newfoundland's rugged coast, he reached a wide gulf – the Gulf of Saint Lawrence – but he didn't believe it would lead him to Asia, so he sailed home. On his second trip, he sailed up the Saint Lawrence to Stadacona (today's Quebec). Ignoring the Native Americans who lived there, he set up camp and took some boats upriver to Hochelaga. Some locals had once told him about Saguenay, an area further west, rich in gold. But when Cartier climbed 'Mont Réal' ('Royal Mountain'), he saw that rapids barred the way. It wasn't long afterwards that winter fell, and 25 men in the French camp died of scurvy. Many more French settlers perished on Cartier's third expedition.

The Indians were probably teasing Cartier about Saguenay because he never found it. The 'diamonds' and 'gold' he did find turned out to be worthless quartz and iron pyrites – fool's gold.

After Cartier's expeditions, the French produced revised maps showing the new French territory, which they called 'Canada'. In fact, 'Canada' is a Native American word meaning 'village'.

*Map labels:* ADA · Atlantic Ocean · Newfoundland · Gulf of St Lawrence · Stadacona (Québec) · Hochelaga (Montreal City)

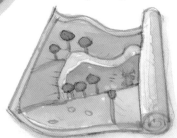

## CARTIER SPARKED FRENCH INTEREST IN CANADA, A LAND RICH IN FISH AND FUR.

**1541** The Spaniard De Soto discovers the Mississippi River.

**1542** The Portuguese adventurer Da Mota becomes the first European to visit Japan.

**1546** Famous cartographer Gerardus Mercator says that the Earth has a magnetic pole.

27

Richard Chancellor

# Richard Chancellor 1556

Sailing for the Company of Merchant Adventurers, Commander Hugh Willoughby and his second-in-command Richard Chancellor sailed from London's River Thames in May 1553. Their brave plan was to try to find a Northeast Passage to Cathay (China) by sailing around the top of Asia. However, their ships were quickly separated by Arctic storms. Willoughby carried on sailing to the island of Novaya Zemlya and then turned for home, but his ships became ice bound. Some Russian fishermen found his frozen remains along with his crew the following spring. Chancellor fared better. He reached the White Sea port of Archangel in Muscovy (Russia), then trekked over a thousand kilometres by sled to pay a visit to the Russian ruler, Tsar Ivan, in Moscow. Ivan agreed to trade Russian goods, like fur, hemp and tallow, in exchange for English metals and wool cloth. Unfortunately, Chancellor was not so lucky on his next Moscow trip: his ship was wrecked off the coast of Scotland, and he was lost for ever along with his precious cargo.

Stephen Burroughs went on Chancellor's 1553 expedition, and named the 'North Cape' – a towering cliff in northern Norway. In 1570, Stephen's brother William included the cliff on his new map.

Chancellor drowned when his ship was wrecked off the coast of Scotland. The Russian Ambassador Nepeja, who was travelling with him, made it to shore, only to be taken hostage by the local Scots.

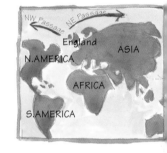

Spain and Portugal controlled all southern routes to the East, so English traders had to find northern ones: either a 'Northwest Passage' over the top or through North America, or a 'Northeast Passage' around the top of Asia.

## CHANCELLOR ESTABLISHED TRADE LINKS BETWEEN ENGLAND AND RUSSIA.

**1550s** Tsar Ivan IV of Russia invades and colonizes new territory in Siberia.

**1551** The Company of Merchant Adventurers is set up by Sebastian Cabot and his investors to compete with the Spanish and establish trade links with the East.

# 1535 Martin Frobisher 1594

The English explorer Martin Frobisher tried to reach Cathay (China) by sailing in a northwesterly direction. But like many seafarers before him, he seriously underestimated the distances involved. When he reached Baffin Bay in today's Canada he mistook it for a short seaway to Asia, and he called the local Inuit people 'Men of Cathay'. The Inuits gave Frobisher and his crew sealskin coats and bearskins in exchange for English bells and mirrors. They also gave Frobisher some black ore, which he took home to Queen Elizabeth. The Royal experts said the ore was gold, and Frobisher returned to get some more. In fact, it was only fool's gold. The bankers who had invested in the 'Cathay Company' lost every penny.

As a young man, Frobisher was a privateer, which really meant he was a pirate. He attacked Spanish ships and stole their cargoes as they sailed home from the New World.

Frobisher's men were fascinated by the Inuit (Eskimos), particularly by the way they made clothes, shelters and boats with sealskin, ate raw meat, and trained their wolf-like dogs (huskies) to pull sleds.

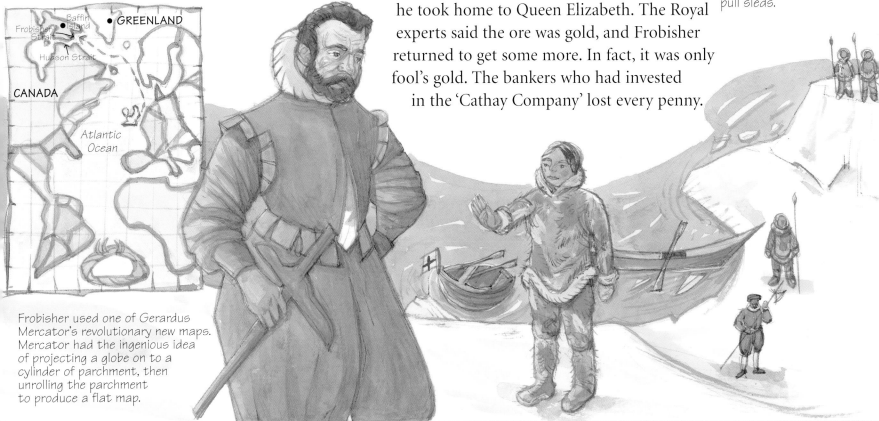

Frobisher used one of Gerardus Mercator's revolutionary new maps. Mercator had the ingenious idea of projecting a globe on to a cylinder of parchment, then unrolling the parchment to produce a flat map.

## FROBISHER TRIED TO FIND A NORTHWEST PASSAGE TO THE EAST.

**1570** Japan opens its port, Nagasaki, to foreign trade.

**1572** Danish astronomer Tycho Brahe finds a new star in the Milky Way – a 'supernova' (exploding star) as bright as Venus.

# c1540 Francis Drake 1596

For most of the the 16th century, Spain and England were deadly enemies. England's Queen Elizabeth I therefore gave her full support to English buccaneers like Francis Drake, who made a fortune out of raiding enemy Spanish ships and Spanish territory overseas. Elizabeth sent the adventurer on his most famous voyage in 1577. Of the five ships, his alone – the *Golden Hind* – made it through the Magellan Strait to the Pacific. When storms swept them back south of Tierra del Fuego, Drake and his crew became the first to round Cape Horn. Afterwards they headed north, up the Pacific coast. The *Golden Hind* was soon groaning under the weight of gold and maps stolen from Spanish ships. Near San Francisco, Drake claimed 'New Albion' (New England) for their Queen, before crossing the Pacific and Indian Oceans, rounding Africa, and sailing back to England. In three years, he had travelled nearly 58,000 kilometres. Elizabeth rewarded him with a knighthood.

**Triangle of Trade**

Drake sold goods in Africa and bought slaves with the profit. Then he sold the slaves to Spaniards in the Caribbean, paying for cotton and sugar to sell back in England.

Voyages of discovery were expensive, and raiding Spanish ships was one way of paying for them. During his circumnavigation, Drake made a 5,000% profit for his sponsors.

Drake helped defeat the invading Spanish Armada in 1588, earning himself the Spanish nickname 'El Draque' (the dragon). Still fighting the Spanish, he died of dysentery in 1596, near Panama.

## SIR FRANCIS WAS THE FIRST ENGLISHMAN TO CIRCUMNAVIGATE THE GLOBE.

**1570** Ortelius makes the first world atlas, with 53 maps.

**1571** Spain and Venice defeat Islamic Turks in the sea battle of Lepanto.

**1571** The Spanish take control of Manila in the Philippines.

**1575** Humphrey Cole makes a Mariner's Astrolabe for Drake to help him navigate.

# 1552  Walter Raleigh  1618

The legend of El Dorado – the city of gold that Raleigh was looking for – comes from an old story about a South American ruler, who coated his body in gold dust before diving into a sacred lake. El Dorado means 'the Golden One' in Spanish.

*Roanoke Island*

As a personal favourite of Queen Elizabeth I, Walter Raleigh was granted a licence to explore North America in 1584. Raleigh himself preferred to stay at home, but he sent two able captains to seek out good land to colonise. Barlowe and Amadas sailed to a wooded and fertile island on America's east coast – Roanoke Island – and amazed Court audiences by bringing back two Alonquin Indians, as well as some tobacco and potato plants. Raleigh's new territory in America was called Virginia in the Virgin Queen's honour. But his plans to set up a colony on Roanoke were fraught with difficulty. The first group of 300 settlers had to be rescued by Francis Drake from attacking Spanish ships; the next 100 disappeared without trace.

By 1595, Raleigh had fallen out of the Queen's favour. To make amends, he set out in search of the fabled city of 'El Dorado' in South America. But after 15 days sailing up Venezuela's Orinoco River, he still hadn't found this gold-rich land. Elizabeth I's successor, James I, ordered him to try again in 1617. Unfortunately, the second expedition was as disastrous as the first. Raleigh returned in disgrace, and was executed.

N. AMERICA
Roanoke Island
Virginia
Venezuela
Orinoco River
S. AMERICA

Raleigh's attempts to set up a colony in America were probably doomed from the start. The English and Native Americans were uneasy neighbours; wild animals ate the settlers' seeds; clean water was hard to come by; and, all alone in an unfamiliar environment, the settlers had too few skills and supplies.

← Tobacco plant

## RALEIGH DREAMED OF SETTING UP THE FIRST ENGLISH COLONY IN AMERICA.

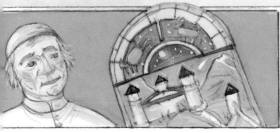

**1582** Pope Gregory XIII introduces a new 'Gregorian' calendar.

**1588** The Spanish send a huge fleet (the Armada) to invade England.

**1596** Tomatoes are brought to England for the first time.

# 1563  Jan Huygen van Linschoten  1611

For most of the 16th century, the Dutch depended on Portuguese traders to import Eastern goods and spices for them. But when Portugal fell under Spanish rule in 1580, Holland saw its chance to break Portugal's control over Eastern trade and build up its own trade links. The Dutch merchant van Linschoten helped lay the groundwork. In 1583, he got a job as a clerk to the Portuguese archbishop in the Indian city of Goa, the centre of Portugal's trading empire. He spent the next five years travelling around the region, gathering valuable information on the Eastern ports and shipping routes, and secretly copying out Portuguese books on navigation.

*Still fascinated with the Orient, in 1594 and 1595 Linschoten accompanied Willem Barents on two expeditions in search of the Northeast Passage, but ice blocked their way.*

ASIA

Japan

China

India

• Goa

• Macao

*In his book Itinerario, Linschoten described his journeys in the East. He also included accounts from a fellow countryman nicknamed 'Dirck China', who worked on the Portuguese merchant ships that sailed from Indian ports to China and Japan.*

When he got back home to Holland in 1589, Linschoten wrote up all his findings in a book called *Itinerario* ('Travel Record'). His excellent notes and maps gave Holland the knowledge it needed to establish its own Eastern trading empire, which eventually became as great as Portugal's.

## LINSCHOTEN HELPED HOLLAND BUILD TRADE LINKS WITH THE EAST.

PORTUGAL

Lisbon  SPAIN

**1580** Portugal comes under Spanish rule.

AFRICA

Guinea

**1595** The Dutch set up a trading post in Guinea, on Africa's west coast.

AFRICA

• Mauritius

**1598** The Dutch set up a small colony on the island of Mauritius in the Indian Ocean.

# c1540 Cornelius Houtman 1599

Frederik Houtman

Like Linschoten, Houtman knew the best way to establish independent trade links with the East was to learn from the Portuguese. Early on in his career, while working in Portugal on behalf of some Dutch merchants, he and his brother Frederick were arrested trying to steal secret Portuguese maps showing Eastern sailing routes. The Dutch traders, who by this time had formed the 'Company of the Far East', paid for their release. Then they ordered Houtman to take four ships to the Spice Islands (the Moluccas) to set up trade links. Using Linschoten's maps, Houtman was able to navigate successfully, and by 1596, was already signing trade agreements in Java, Sumatra and Bali. Back home, he showed the Company his small cargo of cinnamon, cloves, pepper and nutmeg. The goods didn't make the merchants much money at the time, but the deals Houtman had secured promised great riches for the Dutch in the future.

The Dutch eventually joined all their fleets together. The new 'United Dutch East India Co.' was based in Batavia (now Jakarta), and controlled all trade with the Spice Islands.

On a second voyage in 1599, Cornelius was killed in a battle with the Sultan of Atjeh near Sumatra.

His brother Frederik was taken prisoner and remained in Atjeh for several years. He became so fluent in the local language that, back in Holland in 1602, he compiled the first Malay dictionary.

**HOUTMAN'S VOYAGES MARKED THE START OF A 300-YEAR TRADING RELATIONSHIP.**

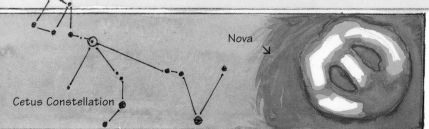

Cetus Constellation
Nova

**1590** Korean astronomers observe a 'nova' – an intensely bright star – in the Cetus constellation.

INDIA

**1594** James Lancaster, English navigator, breaks the Portuguese trade monopoly with India.

# c1550 Willem Barents 1597

In 1871, a Norwegian whaler found the Saved House. It still contained many of the crew's possessions, including etchings, cloth, pewter candles and crockery.

In 1594, a group of merchants from Amsterdam asked Barents to go in search of a Northeast Passage to China. His first two voyages were brought to an end when ice blocked their way, but he chose a more northerly route on his third attempt. This time he charted Bear Island and Spitzbergen, two islands within the Arctic Circle. Then disaster struck: in the frozen sea north of the Novaya Zemlya islands, ice began to crush Barents' ship. To save themselves, the men gathered their supplies and scrambled ashore. They built a driftwood house, which they called 'The Saved House', complete with a steam bath in a barrel, a stove, a chimney, and a crow's nest. But it was bitterly cold and the walls were soon coated with ice. One crewman died of starvation during the winter. The survivors knew they had to leave the island and find help. They set out in June 1597, in two open boats, on a journey that was to cover 2,000 kilometres. "Every minute of every hour we saw death before our eyes," recalled one crewmember. Barents died of scurvy, but the others eventually reached the Kola Peninsula east of Finland, where a waiting ship took them back to Holland.

Gerrit de Veer wrote a journal during the expedition, and published it on his safe return in 1598. He and his companions lived through an Arctic winter, which means they experienced three months without daylight.

NORTH POLE

Arctic Circle

Spitzbergen

Novaya Zemlya

Bear Island

Barents Sea

Kara Sea

Kola Peninsula

RUSSIA

## BARENTS SEARCHED FOR AN ARCTIC SEA ROUTE TO ASIA.

**1595** The Dutch colonize the East Indies.

**1596** Visunsin, a Korean admiral, develops an ironclad warship.

# 1567 Samuel de Champlain 1635

The French naval captain, Samuel de Champlain, led several expeditions to Canada. He became a good friend of the Hurons – a tribe of Native Americans who lived there – and was the founder and first Governor of 'New France' (the French territory in Canada). Champlain's first voyage in 1603 followed Jacques Cartier's route to Hochelaga (Montreal). He also explored the Saint Lawrence River, sailing downstream along the Saguenay and Richelieu, two of its smaller branches.

On a larger expedition, in 1604, Champlain founded Port Royal, the first French colony. His deeply held respect for the Native Americans was rewarded when the Hurons guided him to what became known as Lake Champlain, and later to Lake Ontario and Lake Huron.

CANADA
St Lawrence River
Saguenay River
Port Royal
Lake Huron
Richelieu River
Lake Superior
Lake Champlain
Lake Ontario

De Champlain once sided with the Hurons against a rival Indian tribe, the Iroquois. Remembering this, the Iroquois later sided with Britain in its battles and wars against France.

The French trappers traded the furs of beavers and martens at trading posts. They also sent many back to France, where they were sold at high prices.

## GOVERNOR CHAMPLAIN HELPED ESTABLISH 'NEW FRANCE' IN CANADA.

AMERICA

**1602** The Spanish chart the Californian coast of America.

**1604** England and France sign a treaty about business and trade.

England
Bermuda
Spain

**1612** The English settle Bermuda.

# Willem Jansz c1620

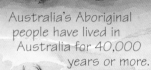

Willem Jansz was an employee of the Dutch East India Company, the powerful company that controlled most of the trade between Europe and the East Indies. Headed for company headquarters in Batavia (today's Jakarta), he left Amsterdam in 1605. Jansz's special mission was to explore trading opportunities east of the Spice Islands. From Batavia, he sailed past Java and Timor, and followed New Guinea's south coast. Then, quite lost, he steered south, and arrived unexpectedly at the northernmost tip of Australia (Cape York). He and his crew stepped ashore on a desert-like headland (Duifken Point) in the Gulf of Carpentaria. But before they had had a chance to explore, they were attacked by a group of Aborigines. Some of the crew were killed, and the others scrambled back on ship. Jansz never knew how historic his landing on Australian soil had been. To the day he died, he believed that he had sailed to a southern part of New Guinea.

Duifken

Australia's Aboriginal people have lived in Australia for 40,000 years or more.

## WILLEM JANSZ WAS THE FIRST EUROPEAN TO REACH 'NEW HOLLAND' (AUSTRALIA).

**1600** England forms its own East India Co. with £70,000.

**1602** The Dutch East India Co. is founded with £540,000!

**1602** Dutch navigator Van Noort completes the fourth circumnavigation of the world.

**1609** The Dutch ship Chinese tea to Europe for the first time.

# c1570 Luis Vaez de Torres c1613

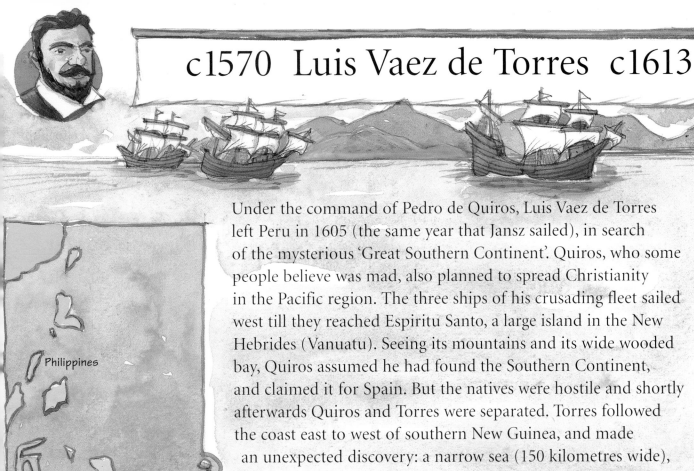

Under the command of Pedro de Quiros, Luis Vaez de Torres left Peru in 1605 (the same year that Jansz sailed), in search of the mysterious 'Great Southern Continent'. Quiros, who some people believe was mad, also planned to spread Christianity in the Pacific region. The three ships of his crusading fleet sailed west till they reached Espiritu Santo, a large island in the New Hebrides (Vanuatu). Seeing its mountains and its wide wooded bay, Quiros assumed he had found the Southern Continent, and claimed it for Spain. But the natives were hostile and shortly afterwards Quiros and Torres were separated. Torres followed the coast east to west of southern New Guinea, and made an unexpected discovery: a narrow sea (150 kilometres wide), full of reefs, separating New Guinea from Australia.

The strait was proof that New Guinea was an island, not part of the vast Southern Continent. However, few heard of Torres' discovery, and the Torres Strait wasn't given its name until the 18th century.

For centuries, European geographers and explorers believed in the existence of a vast 'Great Southern Continent', to balance with landmasses in the Northern Hemisphere. It was Captain Cook who finally proved that the Great Southern Continent was a myth.

OLD WORLD MAP

Imagined vast southern continent

**TORRES DISCOVERED A STRAIT SEPARATING NEW GUINEA FROM AUSTRALIA.**

1608 Dutchman Hans Lippershey invents a refracting telescope.

1609 Galileo builds an astronomical telescope.

# 1580 John Smith 1631

As president of Jamestown's Council, Smith told the townsfolk, "He who does not work, will not eat."

When John Smith was captured by Native Americans, stories say that Pocahontas, Chief Powhatan's 13-year-old daughter, saved the Englishman's life.

Smith wrote several books about the English settlement of America: *True Relation of Virginia* (1608), *Map of Virginia* (1613), and the *General History of Virginia* (1624).

By the early 17th century, Spain had claimed large areas of land in Central and South America. To keep up with the Spanish and encourage English exploration, King James I granted Royal licences to the London and Plymouth Companies, giving them the right to settle territory in North America on his behalf. John Smith joined the London Company. In December 1606, he and his fellow settlers reached Chesapeake Bay, and established Jamestown by the James River. Life was extremely hard for these first settlers. Smith learnt the local Algonquian language and tried to trade with the Native Americans, but they resented the arrival of the English. Narrowly escaping death at the hands of some local deer hunters, Smith eventually decided to leave Jamestown. In 1608, his team travelled 4,800 kilometres, mapping Chesapeake Bay and its rivers. On a later expedition, Smith mapped the coast from Maine to Cape Cod. But he never went back to Jamestown.

## SMITH HELPED SET UP ENGLAND'S FIRST PERMANENT COLONY IN AMERICA.

**1606** The English establish the London and Plymouth Companies to found colonies in Virginia.

**1611** William Shakespeare writes *The Tempest*, a play about a shipwreck.

# c1570 Henry Hudson 1611

The ringleaders of Hudson's mutinous crew all perished during their voyage home to England.

Englishman Henry Hudson's many voyages were attempts to find sea routes to the East – either a 'Northeast Passage' or a 'Northwest Passage'. It was while searching for a Northwest Passage that he famously explored America's northeastern shore. Working for the Dutch, and on the advice of his friend John Smith, he sailed west across the Atlantic in 1609. He reached Nova Scotia and Newfoundland before sailing south to Delaware and Chesapeake Bay, then turned north past Long Island, and found the Hudson River. He sailed up the Hudson for 240 kilometres, hoping to reach the Pacific, until the local Mohawk Indians finally convinced him there was no way through. The following year, with English support, Hudson found a strait that opened into the huge 'Hudson Bay', in present-day Canada. But winter soon set in, and Hudson's ship, the *Discovery* was trapped by ice. Desperate and hungry, the crew finally mutinied, casting their captain, his son and a few sick men adrift, where they died in the thawing ice.

Hudson's reports encouraged the Dutch East India Company to bring fur trappers to the Hudson River. The Dutch trading post on Manhattan Island, established in 1614, eventually became New Amsterdam, then grew into the city of New York.

Hudson Bay

Hudson River

Long Island

Chesapeake Bay

Atlantic Ocean

AMERICA

## HUDSON'S VOYAGES LED TO DUTCH SETTLEMENT OF HUDSON RIVER AREA.

**1611** A brutal but efficient new governor arrives at England's Virginia colony.

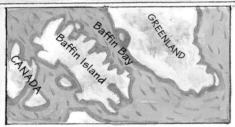

GREENLAND

Baffin Bay

Baffin Island

CANADA

**1616** England's William Baffin discovers 'Baffin Bay' in Canada.

**1616** Dutch astronomer, Snellius, discovers a law of refraction.

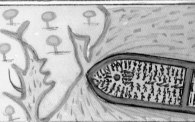

**1619** The first shipment of African slaves arrives in Virginia.

# Dirk Hartog

Dutch sea captain Dirk Hartog was headed for Batavia on the island of Java, when stormy winds swept him too far east. He missed Java completely, which lay to the north, and discovered instead some islands and a long, uncharted coast (western Australia). Dropping anchor in 1616 near the biggest of the islands, now called 'Dirk Hartog's Island', Hartog set off to explore. He was ashore for only three days before concluding that the land was too dry to be any use to his employers, the Dutch East India Company. Australia's western shore eventually became known as 'New Holland' because so many Dutchmen followed Hartog's route. However, the Dutch never considered it a suitable place for settlement. Nor did anyone realise that New Holland lay on the same continent as Duifken Point in North Australia, where fellow countryman, Willem Jansz, had landed in 1605.

The Dutch East India Company, which had its headquarters at Batavia (Jakarta), was formed in 1602. By the time Hartog sailed, the company was powerful enough to insist that only Dutch captains be allowed to explore the coast of New Holland.

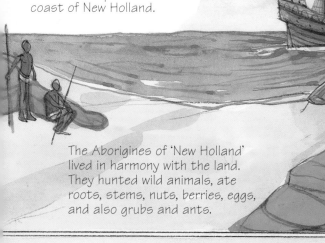

The Aborigines of 'New Holland' lived in harmony with the land. They hunted wild animals, ate roots, stems, nuts, berries, eggs, and also grubs and ants.

## HARTOG WAS THE FIRST EUROPEAN TO LAND ON AUSTRALIA'S WEST COAST.

**1611** England sends its first envoy to India, to see the Great Mogul (Muslim emperor).

**1611** The Dutch begin trading with Japan.

**1619** The Dutch build a fortified port at Batavia in the Spice Islands.

**1620** Dutchman Cornelius Drebb makes a 'diving boat', which is row some distance underwater up London's River Thames.

# c1603 Abel Tasman 1659

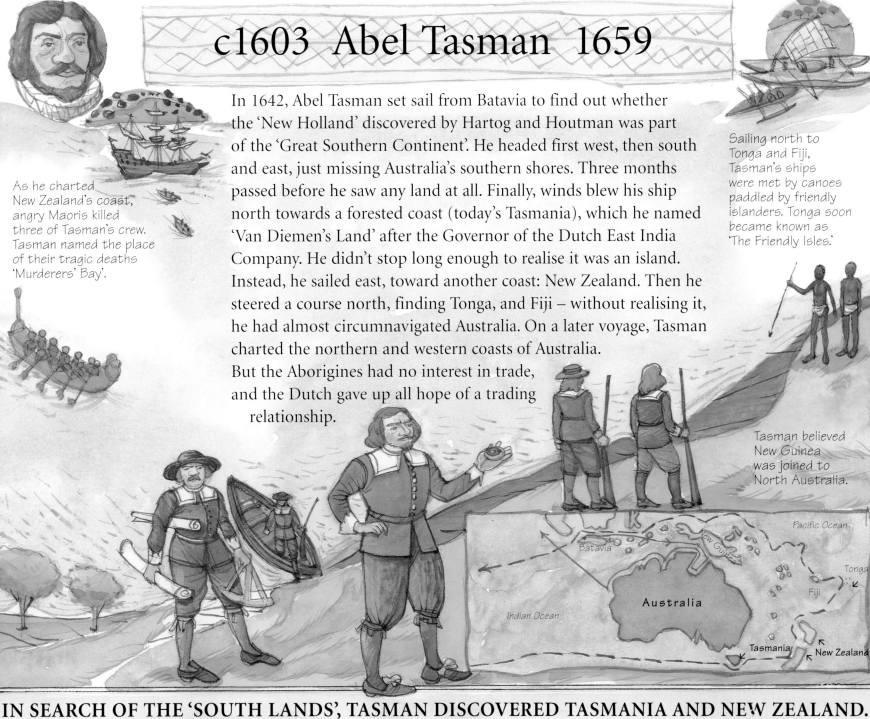

In 1642, Abel Tasman set sail from Batavia to find out whether the 'New Holland' discovered by Hartog and Houtman was part of the 'Great Southern Continent'. He headed first west, then south and east, just missing Australia's southern shores. Three months passed before he saw any land at all. Finally, winds blew his ship north towards a forested coast (today's Tasmania), which he named 'Van Diemen's Land' after the Governor of the Dutch East India Company. He didn't stop long enough to realise it was an island. Instead, he sailed east, toward another coast: New Zealand. Then he steered a course north, finding Tonga, and Fiji – without realising it, he had almost circumnavigated Australia. On a later voyage, Tasman charted the northern and western coasts of Australia. But the Aborigines had no interest in trade, and the Dutch gave up all hope of a trading relationship.

As he charted New Zealand's coast, angry Maoris killed three of Tasman's crew. Tasman named the place of their tragic deaths 'Murderers' Bay'.

Sailing north to Tonga and Fiji, Tasman's ships were met by canoes paddled by friendly islanders. Tonga soon became known as 'The Friendly Isles'.

Tasman believed New Guinea was joined to North Australia.

Pacific Ocean

Batavia

New Guinea

Tonga

Fiji

Australia

Indian Ocean

Tasmania

New Zealand

**IN SEARCH OF THE 'SOUTH LANDS', TASMAN DISCOVERED TASMANIA AND NEW ZEALAND.**

**1640s** Coffee from the New World becomes popular in Paris.

**1642** The great Italian scientist, Galileo, dies.

**1642** A great scientist of the future, Isaac Newton, is born.

# c1605  Semen Dezhnev  1673

Although the straits between Siberia and Alaska are named after Vitus Bering, the Cossack explorer, Semen Dezhnev, found them first. Searching for furs and walrus ivory, Dezhnev explored eastern Siberia for nine years, before arriving at the Kolyma River in 1647. That June, he made a first attempt to explore between the Kolyma and Anadyr Rivers, but his four koches (small sailing ships) hardly got beyond Kolyma's mouth. He tried again in 1648, this time taking a 90-man crew in seven koches. Dezhnev's koch sailed past Wrangel Island and round East Cape, then southwest through an unknown, narrow sea – today's Bering Strait. But it foundered on the Kamchatka coast not long afterwards. Without a ship, Dezhnev was forced to make his way back to the Kolyma overland, When he was finally able to tell the Russian government he'd found a sea passage between Asia and America, they didn't believe him!

East Cape, the most northeasterly point in Asia, is also called Cape Dezhnev.

Siberia · Bering Strait · Alaska

Wrangel Island · East Cape · Bering Strait · Siberia · Kolyma River · Anadyr River · Kamchatka Peninsula

Dezhnev proved that Russia and America were separate. But even now, some of the landmarks he sited in this vast area around Siberia remain unidentified.

## DEZHNEV EXPLORED THE NORTHEASTERN EXTENT OF THE ASIAN CONTINENT.

**1643** Torricelli's new mercury barometer records changes in the weather.

**1647** Johann Hevel completes his Selenographia, a map of the moon's surface.

# c1651 William Dampier 1715

This colourful Englishman was once described as "the mildest mannered man that ever scuttled ship or cut a throat". Falling in with a gang of pirates in 1679, he spent more than a decade sailing round America and raiding Spanish settlements. But Dampier was an explorer, too. He observed the world like a scientist, making careful maps and copious notes. In 1688, he crossed the Pacific, hoping for rich pickings at the Moluccas, and reached Dirk Hartog's New Holland (Australia). The best-selling book he published on his return – *A New Voyage Round the World* – made the British want to find out more about this unknown continent. So, in 1699, sponsored by the British Navy, Dampier sailed again, only this time he was in charge rather than a passenger. Firmly believing that Australia was only a large group of islands, he explored the continent's northwest coast and among the islands of the Dampier Archipelago. Later, when scurvy threatened his crew, he sailed north, discovering what became known as the Dampier Strait. His voyage marked the start of British scientific exploration of the Pacific.

Dampier's ship was found in 2001 near Ascension Island, 300 years after it foundered.

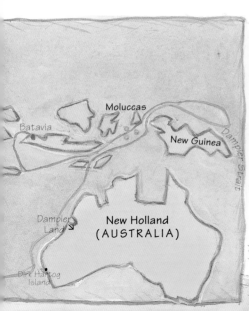

Moluccas
Batavia
New Guinea
Dampier Strait
Dampier Land
New Holland (AUSTRALIA)
Dirk Hartog Island

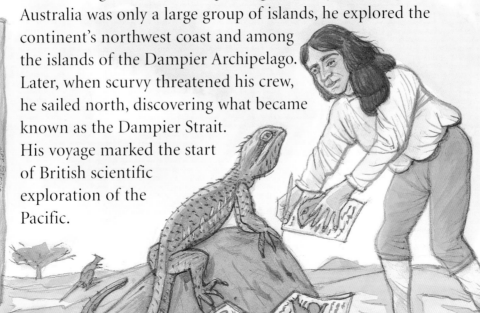

Alexander Selkirk, who sailed with Dampier, asked to be left on Juan Fernandez island off Chile. Years later, in 1708, Dampier went back for him. The story was retold by Defoe as *Robinson Crusoe*. A Meskito Indian on the island was Defoe's 'Man Friday'.

Jonathan Swift also borrowed from Dampier's adventures in strange lands, in his book *Gulliver's Travels*. Dampier is even mentioned in the opening letter, from the fictitious Captain Gulliver to his cousin Sympson.

## DAMPIER WAS THE FIRST ENGLISHMAN TO SET FOOT ON AUSTRALIAN SOIL.

697 In disguise, Tsar Peter the Great of Russia visits Prussia, Holland, England and Vienna.

1701 The pirate Captain Kidd is hanged in England.

1703 Isaac Newton is elected President of the Royal Society.

# 1659 Jakob Roggeveen 1729

Easter Island

Once the Polynesians had carved each *moai* and set it in place, they added eyes and red tufa 'hats'. The *moai* were positioned on rock platforms, which contained graves.

This Dutch admiral was looking for the mysterious 'Great Southern Continent', but found Easter Island instead. Roggeveen sailed to the Pacific in 1721, intending to follow the trade winds, but changeable weather sent him on a roundabout route. He finally anchored ship on Easter Sunday 1722, off a tiny volcanic island. As they prepared to disembark, the Dutch crew gazed in awe at the huge stone figures lined up near the shore. Each one was carved out of the tufa (volcanic rock), and must have weighed many tons. Later, the men watched as some Easter Islanders (who called their home 'Rapa-Nui') built fires in front of the statues and seemed to pray. Roggeveen, however, was more interested in continuing with his journey, and soon ordered the crew back on ship. Although the admiral is best remembered for his discovery of Easter Island, he was only actually there for a day.

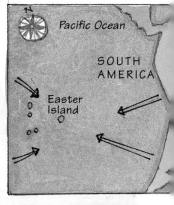

The original inhabitants of Easter Island may have come from South America, or more likely Polynesia, around 400 AD.

## ROGGEVEEN CIRCUMNAVIGATED THE WORLD AND DISCOVERED EASTER ISLAND.

**1700s** Rich Europeans enjoy cultural 'Grand Tours' of Europe.

**1724** Daniel Defoe writes *The Four Years Voyage of Captain George Roberts*.

**1726** Jonathan Swift writes *Gulliver's Travels*, about a castaway's adventures.

**1727** The Quakers, a religious group, demand an end to slavery.

# 1681  Vitus Bering  1741

ASIA  N. AMERICA

Bering Strait

Siberia    Alaska

Mt St Elias

1725 - 30

Kamchatka peninsula

1740 - 41

In 1991, archaeologists found six graves on Bering Island. Forensic experts recreated Bering's face from his skull before reburying the six men.

Vitus Bering caught the eye of Tsar Peter, Russia's ruler, while serving in the Russian navy. The Tsar wanted to know if there was a sea beyond Siberia, dividing Asia and America, and he decided Bering should lead an expedition to find out.

The young Dane left Saint Petersburg in 1725. He trekked overland across Siberia for three years, until he reached the Kamchatka peninsula. From there, with fellow explorer Alexei Chirikov, he took two ships north, and reached what became known as the 'Bering Strait'. If it hadn't been so foggy, they might have seen the coast of America on the other side.

Bering and Chirikov were sent on a second expedition in 1740. This time they sailed eastward from Siberia's Kamchatka peninsula rather than north. They sighted Mount Saint Elias on the American continent (Alaska) on 16 July, 1741. But Bering and his men were already ill with scurvy. On the way back to Siberia, their ship ran aground on a cold, desolate island – now called 'Bering Island'. Bering and half his crew died there. The following summer, survivors took news of the discoveries, and the deaths, back to Saint Petersburg.

Although the straits between Siberia and Alaska take Bering's name, the explorer Dezhnev found them first, almost a hundred years earlier – only the Russian government of the time didn't believe him!

The Bering Strait is 88 kilometres long and 50 metres deep. In ancient times, before the sea levels rose, people and animals crossed the strait using a 'land bridge', which linked the two continents. Native Siberians and Alaskans share similar languages and cultures to this day.

## TSAR PETER SENT BERING ACROSS SIBERIA IN SEARCH OF A ROUTE TO AMERICA.

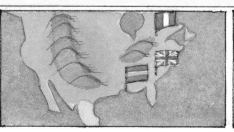

**1720** Russia defeats Sweden in the Great Northern War.

**1720s** Britain, Spain and France establish colonies in America.

**1722** Forward-thinking Tsar Peter sets up an Academy of Science.

**1725** The Delisle family makes accurate maps of Russia.

# 1728 James Cook 1779

James Cook began his working life as a ship's boy and ended his career as 'Captain Cook, famous explorer'. He was a modern, scientific man, with a passion for fact-finding. Unlike many earlier explorers, he wasn't looking to make conquests and win territory, or to forge trade links. He made three great voyages to the Pacific, charting lands from the South Seas to the Arctic, and he ended the mystery of the Great Southern Continent – the landmass that people in Europe believed existed but which had never been found. He collected plants and animals for naturalists to study, and he tried to be friendly with the different peoples he met. Remarkably, considering the epic nature of his voyages, he even kept his crews healthy.

Botanist Joseph Banks found so many plants ashore in Australia that Cook named the place they landed 'Botany Bay'.

Arctic

Pacific Ocean

Antarctic

Botany Bay

New Guinea

Australia

Torres Strait

Cook Strait

New Zealand

## CAPTAIN COOK SAILED THE SOUTH SEAS AND MAPPED THE PACIFIC.

De Bougainville

Bougainvillea

Banksia serrata

Joseph Banks

**1768** De Bougainville, the French navigator, reaches Tahiti and other Pacific islands. The tropical plant Bougainvillea is named after him.

**1769** Botanist Joseph Banks arrives in Tahiti a year after De Bougainville, aboard Cook's *Endeavour*. The tropical plant Banksia is named after him.

Cook made his men eat sauerkraut and cress so that they wouldn't get scurvy, no matter how long they were at sea. Before Cook's time, scurvy killed a third of all sailors.

Cook took Harrison's 1772 chronometer on his second voyage to help navigate. Because it was so accurate, Cook found no difficulty calculating longitude.

Cook encountered Native Americans, Polynesians, Aborigines and Maoris on his travels. The Maoris were the most hostile.

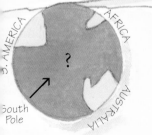

Cook charted 30 Pacific islands during his 1772-75 voyage. He also proved there was no such thing as the 'Great Southern Continent'.

Cook set off on his first adventure in 1768, in a coal ship called the *Endeavour*, headed for Tahiti in the South Seas. His 94-man crew would have been happy to settle on this island paradise, but Cook had secret orders to find the Great Southern Continent. So they sailed on from Tahiti to New Zealand, where Cook charted the 'Cook Strait' between North and South Island. Their next stop was 'Botany Bay' on Australia's east coast. Here they met Aborigines and saw their first kangaroo.

In 1772 Cook set sail once again. This time he headed for the South Polar regions, and became the first person ever to cross the Antarctic Circle. If a Great Southern Continent had existed, Cook would have found it. As he sailed through the icy waters, he sometimes thought that he could see some land in the distance near the South Pole – he was right; this is the continent we now know as Antarctica – but he guessed it would be a cold and unfriendly place to live.

Cook left on his final voyage in 1776, bound for the Pacific and Arctic Oceans. He charted 'Christmas Island' on Christmas Eve. Then, early in 1779, he and his crew arrived in Kealakekua Bay, Hawaii. The friendly islanders offered them gifts and food. However, when a boat went missing, Cook was suspicious and took their king hostage. Suddenly the English sailors were faced with thousands of angry islanders armed with clubs and spears. Cook fired his gun and tried to leave, but he was set upon, and clubbed and stabbed to death.

In the icy Arctic, Cook's crews hauled ice from the sea, melted it and drank the water.

Cook's botanist, Joseph Banks, collected about 400 plants in New Zealand and Australia. He also reported seeing giant sea turtles, and a 'jumping wild dog' (a kangaroo), which the crew cooked and ate.

The Maoris of New Zealand thought English sailors had eyes in the back of their heads because they rowed backwards instead of paddling forwards!

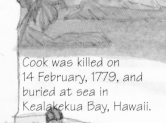

Cook was killed on 14 February, 1779, and buried at sea in Kealakekua Bay, Hawaii.

## HE CLAIMED NEW ZEALAND AND AUSTRALIA FOR BRITISH SETTLEMENT.

**1761** A Danish expedition headed by Castens Niebuhr sets sail for Arabia.

**1761** Lomonosov of Russia identifies a gaseous layer (atmosphere) around the planet Venus.

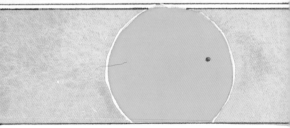

**1768** German naturalist Pallas watches Venus cross in front of the sun as he travels through Russia to China.

# 1769 Alexander von Humboldt 1859

Thomas Jefferson

German scholar Alexander von Humboldt sailed to South America in 1799, on a scientific mission to study Venezuela's rich plant and animal life. He and the French botanist Aimé Bonpland were plagued by mosquitoes as they travelled south across Venezuela's hot, flat grasslands, but they managed to collect thousands of plant specimens to take back to Europe. They also proved that the Orinoco and Amazon Rivers were connected. On their second trip, in 1801, they crossed from Colombia's east coast to Ecuador, and followed the Andes Mountains to Lima in Peru. They collected 30 chests of specimens, watched the volcano Cotopaxi erupting, and climbed Mount Chimborazo. Off Peru's coast, Humboldt made a careful study of the ocean currents (one is named after him). Then he returned to Europe and wrote *Kosmos*, a bestselling five-volume work about nature.

Humboldt met US President Jefferson in 1804. The President was also a keen scientist.

In the interests of science, Humboldt did some dangerous experiments. Once he shocked himself with a Venezuelan electric eel, and another time he drank poison!

Humboldt didn't reach the top of Mount Chimborazo, which is 6,267 metres high, but no one climbed higher for another thirty years.

Cartagena
Venezuela
Colombia  Orinoco R.
Quito
Ecuador  Peru
Lima  Andes  Amazon R.

## SCIENTIST-EXPLORER HUMBOLDT COLLECTED OVER 60,000 PLANT SPECIMENS.

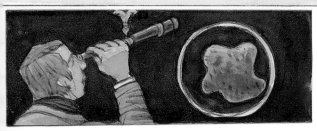
**1801** Giuseppe Piazzi discovers the first asteroid, Ceres.

**1808** Shawnee Indian chief Tecumseh starts campaigning against US expansion in the West.

**1815** William Smith publishes the first large-scale geological map of England.

# 1774 Matthew Flinders 1814

Nicholas Baudin

Flinders was inspired to become a sailor when he read *Robinsoe Crusoe*. Unfortunately, he died on the very day his own travel book, *A Voyage to Terra Australis* was published.

Responding to a request from the British government to make an accurate survey of the coast, Matthew Flinders became the first person to circumnavigate Australia.
It was not the Englishman's first Australian expedition.
He and George Bass had already explored inland from Botany Bay, and sailed round Van Diemen's Land (Tasmania) to prove it was an island.
This time Flinders sailed his ship, the *Investigator*, along the Australian coasts that Captain Cook had missed – the northwest, south and northeast. Two artists and a botanist on board recorded important discoveries. Along the unexplored south coast, Flinders discovered two sizeable inlets: Spencer Gulf, and Gulf Saint Vincent, where the city of Adelaide is now. Then in 1802 he sailed northward to Sydney, and beyond it to the Torres Strait and the Gulf of Carpentaria. His circumnavigation ended back in Sydney in June 1803.

Torres Strait

Gulf of Carpentaria

Australia

Dirk Hartog's Island

Perth
Cape Leeuwin

Spencer Gulf

St Vincent

Adelaide
Melbourne

Sydney
Botany Bay

Tasmania

When Flinders anchored his leaky ship on French Mauritius on his way home, he was arrested as a spy by the French authorities. Flinders was held captive for six years, while the French Commander Baudin claimed all the Englishman's discoveries as his own.

Before Flinders, Europeans had only guessed Australia's shape. The pirate-explorer, William Dampier, thought it was made up of two large islands.

## FLINDERS WAS THE FIRST TO CALL THIS SOUTHERN LAND 'AUSTRALIA'.

NORTH AMERICA
Vancouver

**1793-94** George Vancouver explores America's northwest coast.

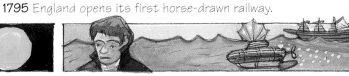

**1795** England opens its first horse-drawn railway.

**1797** MacArthur brings Merino sheep into Australia.

**1800** The astronomer Herschel discovers infrared solar rays.

**1801** Robert Fulton builds Nautilus, the first submarine.

Meriwether Lewis

William Clark

America's President Jefferson bought the huge territory of Louisiana from the French in 1803. Then he asked expert wilderness men, Lewis and Clark, to lead an expedition across it to the Pacific. The president wanted to learn all about this great territory – its wildlife, its geography, and its potential usefulness to his fledgling nation.

Lewis and Clark were well prepared. Clark was a skilful artist and mapmaker, and Lewis was a soldier and expert frontiersman, used to living in wild, open country. He studied botany, zoology and star navigation, especially for the expedition.

## LEWIS AND CLARK PIONEERED THE UNITED STATES' GREAT WESTWARD EXPANSION.

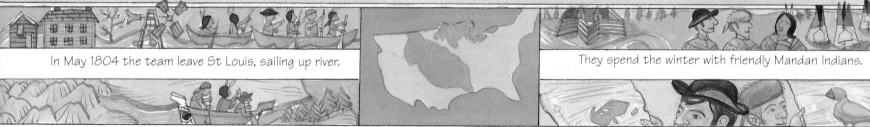

In May 1804 the team leave St Louis, sailing up river.

They spend the winter with friendly Mandan Indians.

Crossing the Rocky Mountains, they head west to the ocean.

The Louisiana territory (in green) between Mississippi and the Rocky Mountains.

As they journey, they map the route and carry out important scientific work.

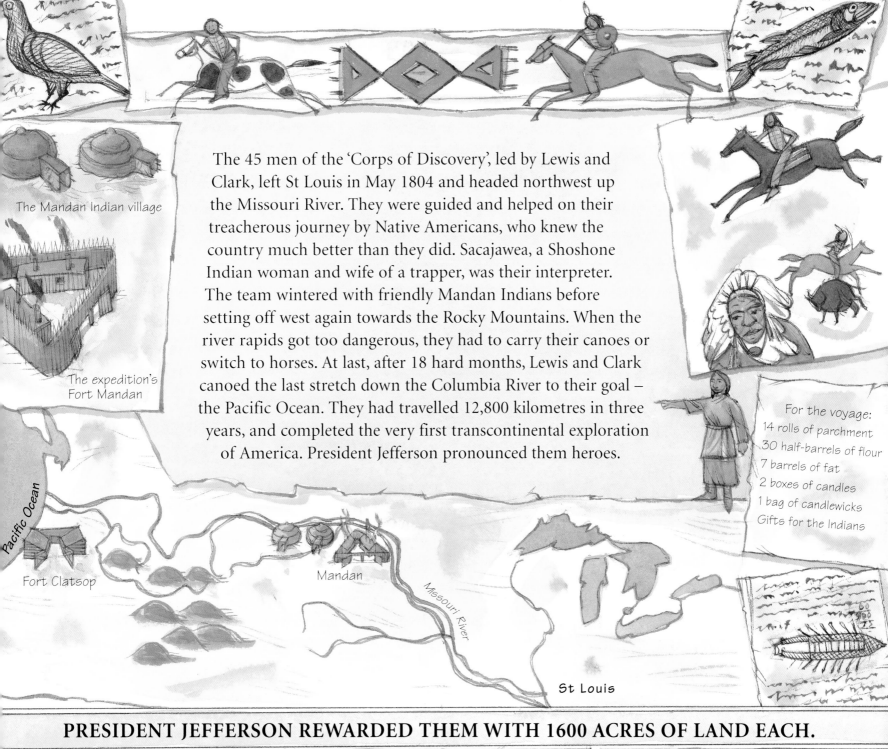

The Mandan Indian village

The expedition's Fort Mandan

The 45 men of the 'Corps of Discovery', led by Lewis and Clark, left St Louis in May 1804 and headed northwest up the Missouri River. They were guided and helped on their treacherous journey by Native Americans, who knew the country much better than they did. Sacajawea, a Shoshone Indian woman and wife of a trapper, was their interpreter. The team wintered with friendly Mandan Indians before setting off west again towards the Rocky Mountains. When the river rapids got too dangerous, they had to carry their canoes or switch to horses. At last, after 18 hard months, Lewis and Clark canoed the last stretch down the Columbia River to their goal – the Pacific Ocean. They had travelled 12,800 kilometres in three years, and completed the very first transcontinental exploration of America. President Jefferson pronounced them heroes.

For the voyage:
14 rolls of parchment
30 half-barrels of flour
7 barrels of fat
2 boxes of candles
1 bag of candlewicks
Gifts for the Indians

Pacific Ocean

Fort Clatsop

Mandan

Missouri River

St Louis

## PRESIDENT JEFFERSON REWARDED THEM WITH 1600 ACRES OF LAND EACH.

**1789-92** Mackenzie crosses Canada. His report inspires Jefferson to explore his own country.

**1803** President Jefferson pays France a meagre $15 million for the huge Louisiana territory.

**1806** Pike completes the exploration of the American West, begun by Lewis and Clark, across the Mississippi.

# 1771  Mungo Park  1806

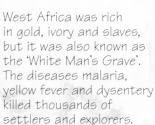

This Scottish surgeon and traveller was sent to West Africa in 1795 to find the great River Niger and legendary city of Timbuktu. Setting out from the mouth of the Gambia River, Park's perilous journey took him through many different kingdoms. On the edge of the Sahara desert he was captured by some Muslim tribesmen, and held hostage for three months. He eventually reached the River Niger on 21 July 1796, and followed it for 500 kilometres before returning to Bamako, and heading west. But by this time Park was dreadfully ill with fever. If it hadn't been for a helpful slave trader, he would never have got home. The British government sent him back to Africa in 1805. Only eight of his original party of forty were still alive when they got to Bamako. In a boat made from two canoes, they drifted down the Niger but they never reached the sea. Their boat was attacked by local tribesmen at the Bussa Rapids, and they all drowned.

Park discovered that the Niger flowed east at Segou. Prior to his expedition, mapmakers had thought that the Niger – which is 4,720 km long – might lead to the Nile or Congo Rivers.

West Africa was rich in gold, ivory and slaves, but it was also known as the 'White Man's Grave'. The diseases malaria, yellow fever and dysentery killed thousands of settlers and explorers.

## PARK WAS THE FIRST EUROPEAN TO REACH AFRICA'S NIGER RIVER.

**1792** Denmark becomes the first country to abolish slave trading.

**1794** France abolishes slavery in its colonies.

**1807** Slavery is abolished in the British Empire.

**1808** America bans the importation of slaves.

# 1788    Hugh Clapperton    1827

Like Park, Hugh Clapperton was Scottish, and met his death while exploring West Africa and the Niger River for the British. From Tripoli, a port on Africa's north coast, some local guides led him and his fellow-explorers Denham and Oudney south across the parched Sahara Desert. Sandstorms, heat and bandits were constant dangers. In February 1823, the party finally reached Lake Chad, a huge expanse of freshwater, which they could see had no direct connection with the River Niger. Denham stayed behind to study the lake while Clapperton and Oudney continued west. On a later expedition, Clapperton and his servant Richard Lander crossed the Niger, and marvelled at the Bussa Rapids where Park had drowned years before. But like Park, Clapperton never got to follow the Niger down to its mouth at the Gulf of Guinea (on the coast of West Africa). He was killed by local tribesmen before he got the chance.

Denham explored the land south and east of Lake Chad. He could see that the lake varied greatly in size between the dry and rainy seasons.

Lake Chad

In 1830, Richard Lander and his brother John finally sailed down the last 800 km of the Niger to the sea, proving that it was not connected to the River Nile.

**CLAPPERTON TRIED IN VAIN TO TRACE THE ROUTE OF THE NIGER.**

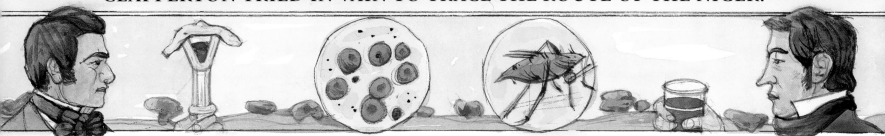

1820 French physicians Pelletier and Caventou discover the drug quinine. Extracted from the bark of the South American cinchona tree, quinine is used to treat malaria, a disease which once killed many European explorers of Africa.

# 1799   Jedediah Smith   1831

Davy Crockett   James Bowie

Although trading routes like the 'Old Spanish Trail' and the 'South Pass' over the Rocky Mountains were well known to the Native Americans, the fur trapper Jedediah Smith – also known as 'Knight of the Buckskin' – rediscovered them for white settlers. His pioneering journeys opened up whole new areas in America's West.

Smith's first overland expedition, in 1826, took him to the Great Salt Lake, in today's Utah, and across the Colorado River and Mojave Desert to California. He was thrown in jail, but managed to escape to lead his companions north through the San Joaquin Valley. The brave party continued across the Sierra Nevada Mountains into the blistering heat of the Great Basin, where they buried themselves in the sand to stay cool. On his next expedition, a year later, Smith reached the Sacramento and Columbia Rivers, before heading east over the Bitterroot Mountains. No one knows for sure, but it seems likely he was eventually killed by tribespeople, while travelling the Santa Fé Trail.

Davy Crockett and James Bowie, famous for his double-edged 'Bowie knife', were well known adventurers of Smith's time. Both died fighting Mexico for Texan independence, at the Battle of the Alamo in 1836.

A grizzly bear attacked Smith on one expedition, smashing his ribs and tearing off his scalp. Fellow explorer Jim Clyman had to sew Smith's ear back on.

Map labels: USA, Columbia R., Colorado R., Bitterroot Mtns, a pass, Sacramento R., Great Salt Lake, Sierra Nevada, ROCKIES, GREAT BASIN, Santa Fé Trail

## SMITH WAS THE FIRST WHITE MAN TO REACH CALIFORNIA OVERLAND.

**1819** The US buys Florida from Spain.

Canada, USA, Florida, Mexico

**1820s** Bolívar and San Martín fight for Latin America's independence from Spain.

Spanish Latin America

**1821** Revolutionary aristocrats in Mexico declare independence from Spain.

USA, MEXICO

**1825** Portugal finally recognises former colony, Brazil, as independent.

BRAZIL

**1827** Opening of the USA's public railway.

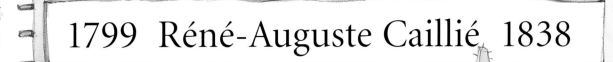

# 1799 Réné-Auguste Caillié 1838

Alexander Gorden Laing

Scotsman Laing was probably the first European to reach Timbuktu, in 1826. He, too, was disappointed by what he saw – just a salt-trading post in barren desert. He was murdered two days after leaving.

In medieval times, Timbuktu was an important trading crossroads between the desert and the coast for salt and West African gold. Tales of the city's great wealth reached Europe and attracted many adventurers, but until Caillé, none had returned.

Disguised as an Arab, this brave Frenchman became the first European to reach Timbuktu, and live to tell the tale. It was a dangerous expedition, even for someone as experienced as Caillé, who lived in French Senegal, and could speak Arabic. His journey began in 1827, in Freetown on Africa's Atlantic coast. Sailing to Conakry, he journeyed inland to Djénne on the Niger River. But Djénne was an unhealthy spot and Caillié caught a fever that set him back four months. It was January 1828 before he was finally able to take a boat-ride to Timbuktu. After all his efforts, the fabled city was a terrible disappointment. Instead of the golden palaces he had expected, he saw only simple mud houses. He left after just two weeks, travelling by camel caravan across the Sahara to Morocco. Back in France, he wrote about his adventures, and claimed a reward for his achievement. He died in 1838 from the tuberculosis he had caught while in Africa.

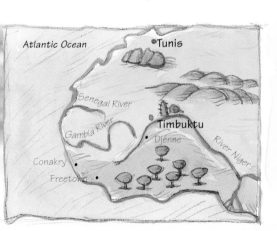

## CAILLIÉ REACHED THE LEGENDARY CITY OF TIMBUKTU IN WEST AFRICA.

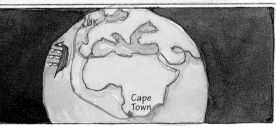

**1820** Thousands of Britons emigrate and settle Cape Colony in South Africa.

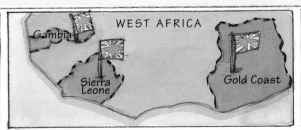

**1821** Sierra Leone, the Gold Coast (Ghana) and the Gambia become part of British West Africa.

**1822** Liberia in West Africa becomes a colony for freed African slaves from America.

# 1777　John Ross　1856

James Clark Ross

The gin distiller, Felix Booth, paid for Ross's second expedition. The Gulf of Boothia and the Boothia Peninsula were named after him.

In 1818, not long after Britain had defeated the French navy at Waterloo, John Ross and William Parry sailed off to look for the elusive Northwest Passage to Asia. They turned back at Lancaster Sound because Ross thought the Crocker Mountains blocked the way. Ross returned in 1829 with his nephew James, aboard the paddle steamer *Victory*. This time they sailed further along Lancaster Sound, then south into the Gulf of Boothia. Their paddle steamer didn't work properly in the Arctic waters so they removed its engine and sailed on, until eventually ice floes stopped them from moving altogether. The men endured for four years in Arctic. Sometimes they left the ship and went on expeditions, using dog-sled teams bought from the local Inuit. They explored the Boothia Peninsula, and James reached the Magnetic North Pole. Eventually, in Spring 1933, they were rescued by a passing whaling ship. When they got back to London, Ross was granted a knighthood.

John Ross's nephew, James Clark Ross was himself a great explorer. During his famous Antarctic expedition, he charted the Ross Sea, Victoria Land, two volcanoes and the Ross Ice Shelf.

Early explorers believed that the North Pole and the Magnetic North were one and the same. In fact, the Magnetic Pole – the point to which a compass needle points – wanders about 10 km every year as the Earth experiences magnetic changes.

Greenland

Lancaster Sound

Davis Strait

Boothia Peninsula

Gulf of Boothia

King William Island

Arctic Circle

Canada

## ROSS PIONEERED MODERN EXPLORATION OF THE CANADIAN ARCTIC.

**1838** Passenger steamships *Sirius* and the *Great Western* sail between England and New York.

# 1795  Charles Sturt  1869

When Charles Sturt set out on his first Australian expedition, in 1828, he was looking for new pastureland for British settlers. The bogs and weeds he found instead were a disappointment. Far more precious was his discovery of the salty, fast-flowing Darling River. He returned the following year to find out more about the river system. On this expedition, he and his team reached the point where the Darling meets the swift current of the Murray, and had to escape from fierce aborigines, before drifting down to Lake Alexandria, near Adelaide. Unable to reach the coast, they then rowed 1,440 kilometres back upstream.

Sturt's most ambitious expedition took place in 1844, when he and 15 others left Adelaide headed for the very centre of Australia, in search of an inland sea. After following the Murray and Darling to Menindee, they journeyed on to Cooper Creek further north. But after 18 months spent in harsh desert land, they had to admit defeat.

The British settlers who arrived in Eastern Australia in the 1820s only explored their immediate area. They hoped that the undiscovered interior would reveal fertile land and fresh water.

### AUSTRALIA

In fact, the remote 'Outback' of central Australia was hot, dry and inhospitable, at least to Europeans. The native Aborigines had been surviving off the land for centuries.

**Map labels:** Simpson Desert, Brisbane, Cooper Creek, Sturt Desert, Darling River, Menindee, Sydney, Murray River, Adelaide, Lake Alexandria

## AS MORE BRITONS SETTLED IN AUSTRALIA, STURT SEARCHED FOR NEW LAND.

1829 The British claim western Australia.

1851 Britain's population reaches nearly 21 million.

# 1809  Charles Darwin  1882

Captain Fitzroy was an able captain, but a difficult and moody man.

"I worked… during the voyage… from a strong desire to add a few facts to the great mass of facts in natural science."

The Englishman Charles Darwin is famous across the world for his theories about evolution, which explain how all living things – plants, animals and humans – change and develop over time. His parents originally planned for him to train as a medical doctor or clergyman, but he hated the sight of blood, and was far more interested in studying plants and animals. After he got his degree from Cambridge University, he answered an advertisement for "an unpaid naturalist of good family"and was soon signed up on a voyage to South America, under the captainship of Robert Fitzroy. Darwin was very excited about the trip, and he was careful to pack plenty of notebooks so that he could note down every single detail of what he saw.

Darwin was influenced by the works of England's great geologist, Charles Lyell. Lyell argued that the Earth was much older than most people thought, and that it had been shaped by gradual – but huge – changes over the course of millions of years.

## SOUTH AMERICA

Galapagos Islands

Brazil

Peru

Rio de Janeir

Chile

Buenos Aire

Argentina

Before he left on the five-year voyage, Darwin had to learn about rocks. He went on a geological tour of Wales, where he realised how easy it is to become confused and miss important facts. He vowed not to let this happen on the HMS *Beagle* expedition.

## DARWIN WAS A BRILLIANT BIOLOGIST AND SKILFUL GEOLOGIST...

**1831** Darwin prepares for the *Beagle* expedition with a trip to Wales.

**1835** Darwin studies finches on the Galapagos Islands.

**1839** Back at home, Darwin writes down everything he has seen in his journal.

**1858** Darwin writes a 35-page article about evolution.

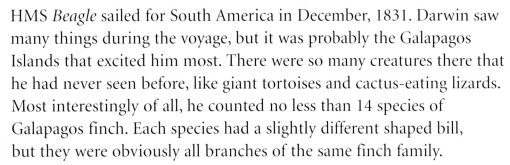

Alfred Russell Wallace collected plants, animals and fossils for museums. He explored the Amazon in 1848.

Darwin wrote books on geology as well as natural history.

In Chile, Darwin was bitten by an insect and became ill. He was troubled with illness for the rest of his life, and some people think this was because the Chilean insect infected him with a disease.

HMS *Beagle* sailed for South America in December, 1831. Darwin saw many things during the voyage, but it was probably the Galapagos Islands that excited him most. There were so many creatures there that he had never seen before, like giant tortoises and cactus-eating lizards. Most interestingly of all, he counted no less than 14 species of Galapagos finch. Each species had a slightly different shaped bill, but they were obviously all branches of the same finch family.

Darwin carried on thinking about the finches for many years. It seemed to him that the 14 types were all descended from one single finch species. Over a very long time, different species had developed – each with a bill best suited to eating the type of food available in the area where it lived. Darwin believed that the finches that had adapted most successfully to their environment were the ones that would survive in the future, because their babies would inherit their useful bills. At the same time, Nature would make sure that the finches with poorly adapted bills would eventually die out.

But if Darwin's Theory of Evolution was correct, the Creation story in the Bible, which says that God took six days to create the world and all living things, must be wrong. Some people were outraged when they realised Darwin was suggesting that humans were descended from a branch of the ape family, and not from Adam and Eve as they had always believed.

Darwin was interested in English nature as well. He studied barnacles, worms, plant reproduction, and was fascinated by dog breeding.

When the Beagle stopped at Tierra del Fuego, Captain Fitzroy dropped off three Fuegans, who he had met during a previous voyage and taken back to England. The Fuegans soon lost their English ways.

In Brazil, Darwin saw what terrible lives the African slaves had to endure. He argued against slavery for the rest of his life.

## ...BUT HE WAS FEARFUL OF PEOPLE'S REACTION TO HIS THEORIES.

**1858** Darwin and Wallace's theories are read aloud at a scientific society meeting.

**1859** Darwin publishes his ideas in *On the Origin of Species*.

**1860s** Darwin studies orchids and domestic plants and animals.

**1871** *The Descent of Man* is published, which extends Darwin's earlier theories to humans.

# 1813  John Charles Frémont  1890

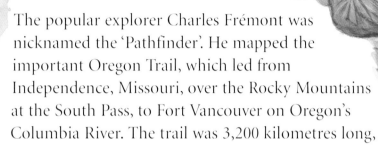

The popular explorer Charles Frémont was nicknamed the 'Pathfinder'. He mapped the important Oregon Trail, which led from Independence, Missouri, over the Rocky Mountains at the South Pass, to Fort Vancouver on Oregon's Columbia River. The trail was 3,200 kilometres long, took about six months by wagon, and was followed by thousands of settlers during the mid-1800s. To encourage even more people to make the journey, the United States government published Frémont's descriptions of the rich, fertile land he had seen. In 1843, he wrote, "The soil of all this country is excellent, admirably adapted to agricultural purposes, and would support a large population." But Frémont didn't always stick to the path. On the way back from his 'Second Topograpical Expedition', he went against the advice of the Native Americans in the area and took a more southerly route. Although it was mid-winter, he climbed more than 3,000 metres over the Sierra Nevada mountains.

Frémont's wife, Jessie, helped him design a special US flag for his mapping expeditions in areas which both Mexico and the US claimed to own. It included a Native American pipe of peace.

Frémont was a politician as well as an explorer. In 1850, he joined California's resistance to Mexican rule, becoming one of the state's first senators. He also ran for the post of America's first Republican Party President, but was unsuccessful.

## FRÉMONT OPENED UP A MAJOR PIONEER ROUTE TO AMERICA'S WEST.

**1842** Britain and the US sign a treaty agreeing on the eastern end of the US-Canadian border.

**1845** Florida and Texas become states of the USA.

**1846** Britain gives up the state of Oregon to the US.

**1846** The western line of the US-Canadian border is agreed.

**1846** Mexico and the US go to war over disputed territory.

**1848** California's Gold Rush begins.

# 1798  Charles Wilkes  1877

Flying the flag for the United States, naval officer Wilkes explored unmapped waters in the Antarctic between 1838 and 1842. As well as boosting his country's knowledge of the South Seas, it was a chance to search out new hunting ground for their whaling industry. The crew of his six-ship expedition included oceanographers, botanists, naturalists and geologists. They mapped mountains and headlands, and found an emperor penguin with pebbles in its stomach – proving that there had to be land under all the ice. Wilkes himself discovered and named a huge cliff of ice, 'Termination Land'. He also made a few mistakes, thinking some ice walls were land when they were not. Worse, ice tore the rudder off one ship, the *Peacock*, and another, the *Sea Gull*, disappeared mysteriously off Chile's coast. On his return, Wilkes was charged with being too strict with his crew, many of whom deserted.

The huge volume of ice that covers the Antarctic continent amounts to 80% of the Earth's fresh water, and is as much as 4 kilometres thick in some places. These days, global warming is melting it dangerously fast.

The British explorer James Clark Ross later claimed to have sailed across areas that Wilkes had mapped as land. Ross was right: Wilkes had been fooled by 'looming' – a trick of the polar light, which makes land look closer than it really is.

Wilkes
Land

ANTARCTICA

Termination
Land (Shackleton Ice Shelf)

Magellan
Straits

## WILKES WAS THE FIRST TO DECLARE ANTARCTICA A CONTINENT.

**1840** Shönbein, a German chemist, discovers ozone.

**1840** Agassiz explains how ice covered the Earth during successive Ice Ages.

**1842** Maury, an American naval officer, studies the oceans.

**1846** The scientific Smithsonian Institution is founded in Washington, USA.

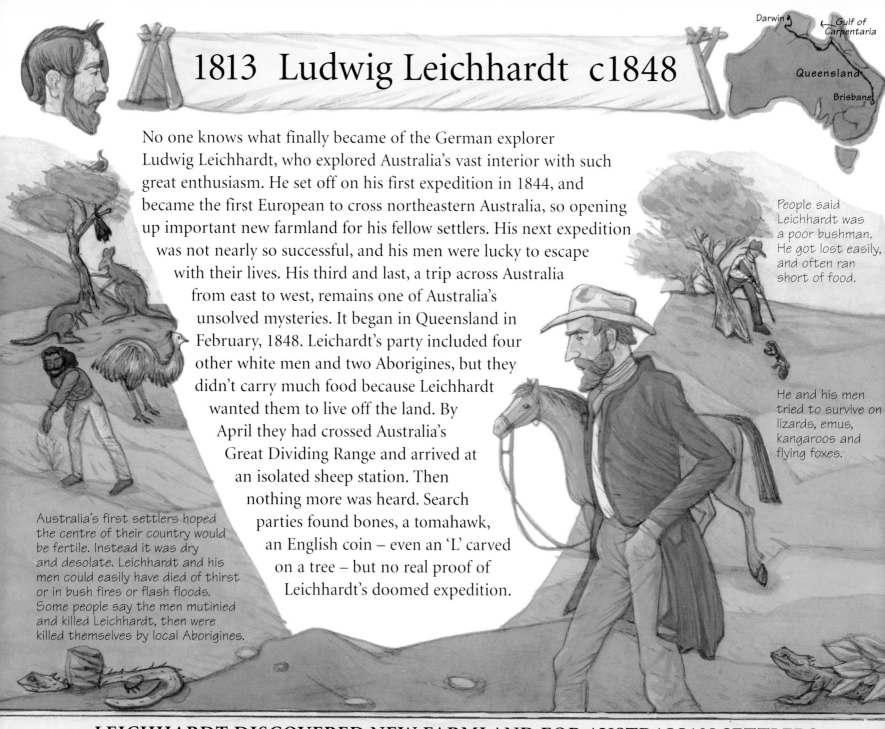

# 1813  Ludwig Leichhardt  c1848

Darwin
Gulf of Carpentaria
Queensland
Brisbane

No one knows what finally became of the German explorer Ludwig Leichhardt, who explored Australia's vast interior with such great enthusiasm. He set off on his first expedition in 1844, and became the first European to cross northeastern Australia, so opening up important new farmland for his fellow settlers. His next expedition was not nearly so successful, and his men were lucky to escape with their lives. His third and last, a trip across Australia from east to west, remains one of Australia's unsolved mysteries. It began in Queensland in February, 1848. Leichardt's party included four other white men and two Aborigines, but they didn't carry much food because Leichhardt wanted them to live off the land. By April they had crossed Australia's Great Dividing Range and arrived at an isolated sheep station. Then nothing more was heard. Search parties found bones, a tomahawk, an English coin – even an 'L' carved on a tree – but no real proof of Leichhardt's doomed expedition.

People said Leichhardt was a poor bushman. He got lost easily, and often ran short of food.

He and his men tried to survive on lizards, emus, kangaroos and flying foxes.

Australia's first settlers hoped the centre of their country would be fertile. Instead it was dry and desolate. Leichhardt and his men could easily have died of thirst or in bush fires or flash floods. Some people say the men mutinied and killed Leichhardt, then were killed themselves by local Aborigines.

## LEICHHARDT DISCOVERED NEW FARMLAND FOR AUSTRALIAN SETTLERS.

**1840s** Karl Hencke discovers the asteroids Astral (1845) and Hebe (1847).

**1848** Scottish settlers arrive in Dunedin, New Zealand.

**1850** Australia's first university is founded in Sydney.

# 1786 John Franklin 1847

During Franklin's earlier expeditions, in 1819 and 1825, he charted most of the coast of Arctic Canada.

In 1845, the British Navy chose Sir John Franklin, one of its most skilful mappers and navigators, to continue the search for a Northwest Passage to Asia, taking an Arctic Sea route north of America. Franklin knew the Arctic well, particularly Canada. He sailed north in May with over 130 men in two navy ships, *Erebus* and *Terror*. Some whalers caught sight of them later near Baffin Bay. Then they seemed to disappear, and no news was heard of them until 1948. In fact, the terrible Arctic winter had closed in and Franklin's ships had become icebound. They survived on the thousands of tins of food they had with them. As soon as summer came they sailed south but, tragically, were soon trapped again by winter ice. By spring 1848, Franklin and another 23 men were dead. The desperate survivors abandoned ship and trudged across Canada's frozen mainland. They all died: some were killed and eaten by their starving shipmates. The local Inuits watched as exhausted crewmembers fell down dead, even as they walked.

The crew's food was probably poisoned by lead as it leaked from the tin casing. The lead would have made the men weak, and unable to think clearly.

**FRANKLIN AND HIS CREW DIED TRYING TO FIND A NORTHWEST PASSAGE.**

**1840** English and French-speaking Canada is united as one province.

**1840** The first regular trans-Atlantic steamship service is launched.

**1845** The Irish potato blight leads to famine and emigration.

**1849** Livingstone crosses the Kalahari Desert in Southern Africa.

# 1821 Heinrich Barth 1865

This German explorer already had extensive experience of travelling in North Africa before he joined a British expedition in 1850. During these earlier trips, he had got to know the local people and taught himself Arabic, so he was well prepared when he set out across the Sahara with expedition leader James Richardson and Adolf Overweg. When Richardson died of a fever, Barth took over his command, and he and Overweg explored the area around Lake Chad. But it wasn't long before Overweg caught a fever and died, too. Battling illness himself, Barth continued alone, and found the Benue River, a tributary of the Niger. He then headed west towards the Niger River and spent ten months in Timbuktu. He observed how the Niger flowed in a great sweeping bend. After re-crossing the Sahara, he finally reached Tripoli in 1855.

Early on in the expedition, Barth climbed the mysterious Mount Idinen, near Ghat, and collapsed from heat and thirst. To revive himself, he opened a vein in his arm and drank his own blood.

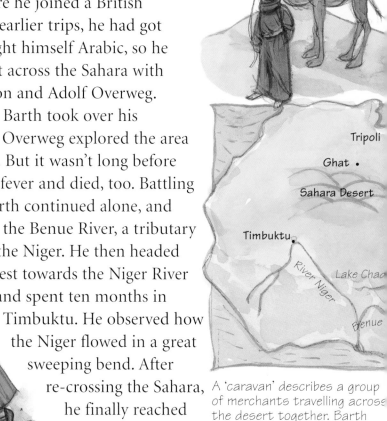

Tripoli

Ghat •

Sahara Desert

Timbuktu

River Niger

Lake Chad

Benue

A 'caravan' describes a group of merchants travelling across the desert together. Barth mapped many of these centuries-old caravan paths, including the eastern route from Tripoli to Lake Chad.

## BARTH TRACED OLD CARAVAN ROUTES ACROSS THE SAHARA DESERT.

**1850** Britain buys Danish trading posts in West Africa.

**1859** French engineer de Lesseps starts building the Suez Canal in North Africa.

**1859** The Spanish invade Morocco in North Africa.

Speke

Burton

# 1821 Richard Burton 1890
# 1827 John Hanning Speke 1864

Lake Albert
Victoria Nile
Lake Victoria
Ujiji • Tabora
L. Tanganyika
Zanzibar

Speke, a British Army officer, and the clever and colourful Burton were determined to find the source of the Nile – the longest river in Africa. They travelled west from Zanzibar, fighting illness all the way, and were the first Europeans to see Lake Tanganyika. Speke continued on alone, leaving Burton to rest at Tabora. When he discovered Lake Victoria, he was sure he had found the source of the Nile, and rushed back to tell Burton. Burton disagreed, saying the true source was Lake Tanganyika. Resolved to discover the truth, Speke returned to Africa in 1860. He remained convinced that the Nile began at Lake Victoria – which it does – but did not persuade Burton and his doubters in England.

Burton spoke around thirty Eastern languages, and was also a soldier, geologist, poet, anthropologist and botanist.

Burton and Speke were fierce rivals. The day before they were due to debate the source of the Nile in Bath, England, Speke shot himself – perhaps accidentally – on a partridge shoot. "The charitable say that he shot himself, the uncharitable that I shot him," said Burton.

Cairo
Red Sea
White Nile
Blue Nile
R. Nile
Lake Albert
Victoria Nile
Lake Victoria
Lake Tanganyika

# THE NILE WAS OF GREAT INTEREST TO EUROPEAN EXPLORERS.

**1860** France and Britain sign a treaty agreeing free trade.

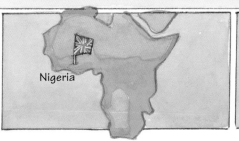
Nigeria

**1861** Britain obtains the coastal area of Nigeria.

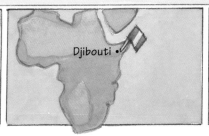
Djibouti •

**1862** France buys an important African port in present-day Djibouti.

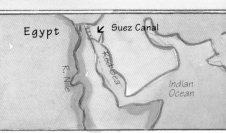
Egypt
Suez Canal
R. Nile
Red Sea
Indian Ocean

**1869** The Suez Canal opens, linking the Indian Ocean, the Red Sea and the Mediterranean.

# 1831　Isabella Bird Bishop　1904

Most 19th-century Victorians believed that women shouldn't travel because they were too weak. But when she wasn't having adventures, Bird Bishop said she felt "dull and inactive".

This great Victorian traveller and writer began travelling at the age of 21, on the advice of her doctor. With just £100 in her pocket, she toured Canada and the United States, and on her return wrote *An Englishwoman in America*. She also made trips to Australia, New Zealand, and Hawaii – where she rode horses like the natives (astride rather than the usual sidesaddle) and climbed volcanoes.

In 1878, before marriage to Dr Bishop temporarily ended her travels, Bird did a short tour of Asia. In the remoter parts of Japan and China, she was often the first foreigner the locals had ever seen. She went back to Asia as a widow in 1888. This time she went riding in the snowy Himalayas and organised two hospital building projects in India. Just before she died, she made a final visit to Africa, and rode across the Atlas Mountains of Morocco.

Despite her sex, Bird Bishop was accepted by the Establishment in the end. In 1892, she became the first woman to be elected a Fellow of the Royal Geographical Society.

## BIRD'S ADVENTURES INSPIRED OTHER WOMEN TO TRAVEL ABROAD.

**1883** The Northern Pacific Railroad is opened in the US.

**1883** The Orient Express opens between Paris and Istanbul.

**1885** Africa's Cape Railway is extended to Kimberley.

**1872** Jules Verne writes *Around the World in 80 Days*.

**1886** The Canadian Pacific Railway opens.

Burke

Wills

# 1820  Robert O'Hara Burke  1861
# 1834  William Wills  1861

When the South Australian government offered a prize for the first south-to-north crossing of Australia, Robert Burke and William Wills decided to take up the challenge. Sadly, although they succeeded, they died before they could receive the reward. Burke's team started out from Melbourne in 1860, with 25 camels to carry supplies. The he and Wills, as his second-in-command, and six others left the main party behind and set off north towards Cooper Creek. When they arrived, Burke sent one of the men back to fetch the others and more supplies. Leaving another man, Brahe, behind in the blistering heat at Cooper Creek, Burke, Wills, King and Gray then headed north again, promising to return in three months. The four men finally reached their destination, the Gulf of Carpentaria, in February, 1861. But they had made a terrible miscalculation: they only had half the supplies needed for the 10-week return journey back to Cooper Creek. Of the four, only King survived to tell the tale.

Struggling south in heavy rain, Gray died first. The three survivors managed to get to Cooper Creek, but Brahe had just left. Ill and confused, they walked in circles until June, when both Wills and Burke died of starvation. King was rescued by Aborgines in the nick of time.

John McDouall Stuart organised a rival south-north crossing of Australia. He left Adelaide in October 1861 and reached Australia's north coast in July, 1862. The government awarded him £2,000 in prize money.

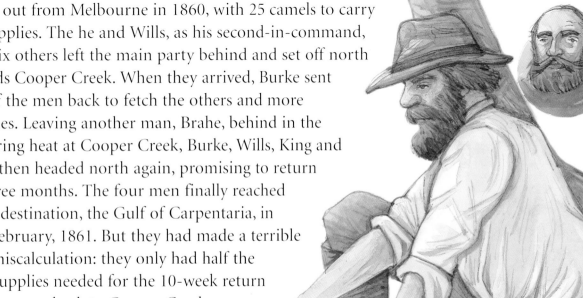

Gulf of Carpentaria

Australia

Cooper Creek

Melbourne

# THE BURKE AND WILLS TRAGEDY SHOCKED AUSTRALIA.

**1861** Charles Dickens writes about an Australian convict, Magwitch, in *Great Expectations*.

**1862** An English cricket team tours Australia for the first time.

**1867** England sends its last shipment of convicts to Western Australia.

# 1842  Peter Kropotkin  1921

Peter Kropotkin brought remote and unknown Siberia into the international spotlight. As he explored this vast region between 1862 and 1865, his fascination grew. He learnt about the structure and development of East Asia's mountain ranges, and compiled a geographic survey of Manchuria for the Russian Geographical Society. The society was so impressed with his work, they offered him an important post. But Kropotkin had seen how cruel the Russian government was to the peasants and exiled prisoners in Siberia, and became an anarchist instead.

Kropotkin was an anarchist – someone who does not believe in government. He was exiled from Russia in 1873, after dedicating his life to social justice.

Lenin          Trotsky

He returned from exile in 1917, at the time of the Russian Revolution, led by Vladimir Ilyich Lenin and Leon Trotsky.

*Map labels: St Petersburg, Moscow, Siberia, Russia, Manchurian Plain, China*

## EX-ARMY OFFICER KROPOTKIN STUDIED THE MOUNTAINS OF SIBERIA.

**1861** Russia's peasants are freed from slavery.

**1864** Rossi writes about the catacombs – Rome's underground burial caves.

**1865** Englishman, Whymper, climbs the Matterhorn.

*Map labels: RUSSIA, Bering Strait, ALASKA, CANADA*

**1867** Russia sells Alaska to America for US$7,200,000.

# 1813  David Livingstone  1873
# 1841  Henry Morton Stanley  1904

Stanley

Livingstone

Livingstone was single-minded. Even though he was mauled by a lion, and suffered terrible fevers, he wasn't put off exploring.

Victoria Falls

AFRICA

Lake Tanganyika

Congo R.

Zambezi R.

Victoria Falls

Kalahari Desert

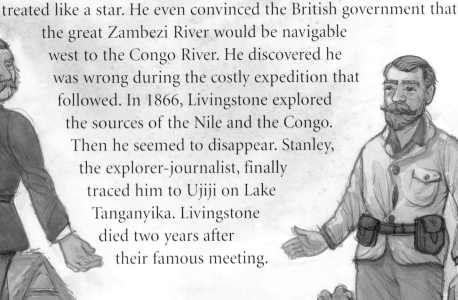

Livingstone arrived in Africa in 1841 to begin work as a Christian missionary, spreading the word of God amongst the African people. He also wanted to get to know the land. He crossed the Kalahari Desert and marvelled at the thunderous Victoria Falls, and in 1856, became the first European to cross Central Africa. When he returned to London, he was treated like a star. He even convinced the British government that the great Zambezi River would be navigable west to the Congo River. He discovered he was wrong during the costly expedition that followed. In 1866, Livingstone explored the sources of the Nile and the Congo. Then he seemed to disappear. Stanley, the explorer-journalist, finally traced him to Ujiji on Lake Tanganyika. Livingstone died two years after their famous meeting.

Like Livingstone, Stanley was a remarkable explorer. On his huge 1874-77 expedition, he crossed the whole of Africa, in 999 days. He also helped Belgium's King Leopold II establish the 'Congo Free State'.

## BY MAPPING ITS INTERIOR, LIVINGSTONE REVEALED AFRICA TO EUROPE.

**1876** King Leopold founds the International Association for the Exploration and Civilization of Congo.

**1877** England's Queen Victoria becomes Empress of India.

**1884** Carl Peters founds a society promoting German colonization.

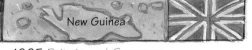

New Guinea

Vietnam

Cambodia

**1884** A Berlin conference triggers the European 'Scramble for Africa'.

**1885** Britain and Germany annexe parts of New Guinea.

**1887** French colonies Vietnam and Cambodia become the Union of Indo-China.

# 1830 Charles Wyville Thomson 1882

*Challenger* was a sailing ship, but it was fitted with a steam engine to help it manoeuvre during scientific experiments. It was equipped with special biology, chemistry and physics laboratories, and plenty of storage space for specimens.

Plankton (magnified)

deep sea sponge ↗

Thomson's team was the very first to be put together for the sole purpose of scientific study of the oceans. Besides himself and his crew, HMS *Challenger* carried three naturalists, a chemist and an artist. Thomson planned their work carefully as they circumnavigated the globe. Each time *Challenger* stopped – 362 times in four years – the team made soundings to calculate the ocean depth. Sometimes they hauled interesting new plants and animals aboard, dredged up from the deep-ocean floor. All the while they noted the weather conditions, ocean-current speed and direction, and the water's salinity and temperature at different depths. Some of their samples could be analysed right there on board, while others were stored safely for examination back in Britain. By 1876, at the end of *Challenger's* 111,000-kilometre voyage, they had enough information to fill 50 volumes with notes and illustrations, which were published between 1880 and 1895.

The deepest sounding Thomson recorded (8,185 metres) was at 'Challenger Deep' near the Marianas Trench. Challenger's new map of the ocean beds also showed a mysterious line of undersea mountains – the Mid-Atlantic Ridge.

Atlantic Ocean

Mid-Atlantic Ridge

Indian Ocean

Mariana Trench

## THOMSON'S EXPEDITION LAUNCHED A NEW SCIENCE: OCEANOGRAPHY.

**1870** The launch of SS *Oceanic*, the first modern luxury liner.

**1872** William Thomson invents a machine to take accurate soundings at sea.

**1875** Matthew Webb becomes the first person to swim the English Channel.

# India's Pundit-Explorers

Kintup

Kishen Singh

Nain Singh

In the 1860s and 1870s Britain and other European powers became very interested in northern India and Himalayan mountain countries like Tibet. Because some of these places were forbidden to outsiders, British governors in India trained local 'pundit-explorers' to carry out surveying work. Courageous and skilful Indians – like Kintup, Nain Singh and Kishen Singh – made secret journeys, disguised as merchants or Buddhist pilgrims. Kishen Singh's expeditions took him from Kathmandu in Nepal to Lhasa, the mysterious capital of Tibet, to Mongolia's Gobi Desert. Nain Singh walked for 10 years, mapping mountains north of the Himalayas and India's Brahmaputra River tributaries. Kintup also studied the the Brahmaputra, and discovered that it and the Tsangpo River in Tibet were one and the same thing.

Kintup's career as an explorer was interrupted when his companion, a Mongolian lama (monk), sold him into slavery. It was two years before Kintup escaped to India.

Pundit comes from the Hindi word meaning 'teacher', which was Nain Singh's first profession.

All the pundit-explorers were taught to walk using 33-inch paces and to keep their sketched maps in Tibetan prayer wheels. They counted their steps on 100-bead Tibetan rosaries – 2,000 paces per mile.

India
Tibet
China
Dehra Dun
Brahmaputra R.
Lhasa
Nepal
Himalayas
Kathmandu
Indus R.

## INDIAN EXPLORERS MAPPED THE HIMALAYAN REGION FOR THE BRITISH.

**1870** The Swede, Nordenskjöld, explores Greenland's interior.

**1873** Payer and Weyprecht discover Franz Josef Land – 60 islands in the Siberian Arctic.

**1877** Italian astronomer Schiaparelli believes he sees artificial canals on Mars' surface.

# 1861  Fridtjof Nansen  1930

In September 1893, the Norwegian scientist and explorer Fridtjof Nansen let his ship, the *Fram*, freeze into pack ice north of Siberia's Lena estuary. He believed that this was the best way to reach the North Pole, because the ice would drift west on the ocean currents towards the Greenland Sea, taking the *Fram* with it. It almost worked – they began to drift westward, but too far south to cross over the Pole. When they realised this, Nansen and his companion Hjalmar Johansen abandoned ship and made for the Pole themselves using dog sleds. They took kayaks, too, and rations for themselves and the dogs. Their bold trek ended just 384 kilometres short of the Pole, further north than anyone had reached before. They arrived back home in Norway in spring 1896, just as their ship and its crew reached Spitzbergen and open water. The *Fram* had been drifting slowly westward for three years, so proving Nansen's theory that polar ice is constantly on the move.

Nansen designed his own lightweight skis, clothing, cooking pots, and 'Nansen sledges'. These lightweight, flexible sledges are still used today.

Nansen was awarded a professorship in oceanography in recognition of his careful scientific observations. But after the First World War he turned his attention to international humanitarian work. He got food to many starving Germans and Russians, and helped refugees and prisoners of war for the League of Nations.

Nansen's interest in ice drift was sparked by the 1881 Jeanette tragedy. This American ship foundered in pack ice off Siberia. The wreck was discovered three years later, off the coast of Greenland.

## NANSEN BASED HIS POLAR EXPEDITIONS ON SCIENTIFIC THEORY.

**1891** Russia begins building a trans-Siberian railway.

**1893** The Corinth Canal opens in Greece.

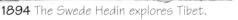

**1894** The Swede Hedin explores Tibet.

**1895** The Kei canal opens, linking the North and Baltic Seas.

**1895** Marconi, from Italy, invents the wireless telegraph.

# 1856  Robert Peary  1920

Frederick Cook

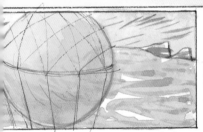
Robert Peary

Matthew Henson

It was Robert Peary, an ambitious American naval officer, who finally made it all the way to the North Pole. He spent many years beforehand exploring Greenland's Arctic ice cap – once with his wife, but mostly with his African-American friend Matthew Henson. During these early expeditions Peary explored Greenland's icy interior further north than Nansen had before him, and proved that it was an island.

In July 1908, Peary set out on his third attempt to reach the Pole. He and his team sailed the *Roosevelt* from America to the north of Ellesmere Island, 640 kilometres from the Pole. They wintered at Cape Sheridan, before beginning their difficult journey across the shifting pack ice from nearby Cape Columbia. Thanks to fine weather and swift sled dogs, they made excellent progress. They arrived at the Pole on 6 April, 1909, only five short weeks after leaving Cape Columbia.

A group of wealthy New Yorkers, who called themselves 'The Peary Arctic Club', helped pay for Peary's expensive polar expeditions.

Peary's rival Frederick Cook, leading a smaller team, claimed to have reached the North Pole a year before Peary, in 1908, but no one believed him. Others have queried Peary's claim – on the grounds that he couldn't have made it to the Pole and back so quickly.

## PEARY ASTONISHED THE WORLD WITH HIS DASH TO THE POLE.

**1902** J. M. Bacon crosses the Irish Sea in a balloon.

**1903** The Wright brothers make the first powered flight.

**1903** Russia's Tsiolkovsky says that rockets could be used to explore space.

**1909** Frenchman Louis Blériot flies his monoplane across the English Channel.

# 1862 Mary Kingsley 1900

*Brycinus kingsleyae*

AFRICA

Ogowe River

GABON → Congo River

Until she was 31, Londoner Mary Kingsley lived at home, caring for her frail mother. She never went to school, but she read her father's books on travel and science, and secretly dreamt of Africa. When her parents died, she was free to make her first African trip, to the Congo River. Kingsley was flouting Victorian convention by travelling without an escort, but she had a commission from a London museum to collect river-fish and study African customs. Some of the fish she brought back were named after her. Two years later, Kingsley paddled up the Ogowe River in Gabon. She met members of the Fang tribespeople, collected more fish, and even climbed Mount Cameroon.

Back home, the adventuress gave interesting and humorous lectures about her West African journeys. She wanted her European audiences to share her respect for the African people. She died of typhoid in 1900, nursing prisoners of war in South Africa.

*Ctenopoma kingsleyae*

## CANOEING DOWN THE CONGO GAVE KINGSLEY A TASTE FOR FREEDOM.

**1890s** European countries scramble to gain African territory.

**1893** Africans rebel against the British South Africa Company in Matabele.

**1894** Rudyard Kipling writes *The Jungle Book*.

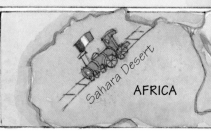

**1898** France tries again to build a railway across the Sahara.

# 1868  Gertrude Bell  1926

**Lawrence of Arabia**
The British soldier and writer, T. E. Lawrence, helped the Arabs rebel against their Turkish rulers. During the 1916-18 campaign, Lawrence consulted Bell's excellent maps of the Arabian desert.

Englishwoman Gertrude Bell only ever felt truly free up mountains or in deserts. She was 22 when she made her first trip abroad, to Tehran, the capital of Iran. The archaeology of the Middle East fascinated her, but her family disapproved of her travels and quickly brought her home. Bell was soon away again, this time exploring the Syrian Desert. She admired the civilized Arabs and their timeless way of life. In turn they respected her, and gave her the name 'daughter of the desert'.

One of Bell's most important achievements was to map new routes between Damascus, Ha'il and Baghdad. The men at London's Royal Geographical Society said women could never be proper explorers, but her expert knowledge of the region and the local languages was invaluable to British Intelligence during the First World War. Tragically, her energies failed her in the end; she took her own life in 1926.

## BELL TRAVELLED DEEP INTO THE ARABIAN DESERT AND STUDIED ANCIENT RUINS.

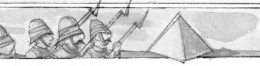

**1882** The British army occupies Cairo.

**1883** Krakatoa in Indonesia is almost destroyed by a volcanic eruption.

**1889** The Suez Canal in Egypt, which links the Mediterranean with the Red Sea, opens to all ships in peace and war.

**1885** The Arabian Nights, a collection of 10th-century folk tales, is translated into English.

**1889** Settlers make a 'land grab' of Indian land in Oklahoma, USA.

# 1872  Roald Amundsen  1928
# 1868  Robert Scott  1912

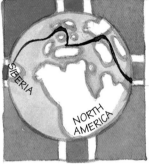

Between 1903 and 1905, Amundsen made the first voyage through the 'Northwest Passage', a sea route north of Canada connecting the Atlantic and Pacific Oceans.

The names Amundsen and Scott are forever joined in history as competitors in the race to the South Pole. The Norwegian Roald Amundsen was the victor, partly because he planned everything so carefully in advance. His route to the Pole was also shorter. Whereas the Englishman had his base at Cape Evans, Admunsen and his team pitched camp at the Bay of Whales. By October 1911, the Norwegians were ready to clip on their skis and begin a trek of 2,250 kilometres across the ice. They used four dog sleds to pull them safely over dangerous crevasses and a high glacier. Triumphant, they reached the Pole on 14 December, 1911, and sat down to a hearty meal.

Scott's team, on the other hand, was beset with troubles from the outset. Their motor sleds broke down, and they discovered too late that their ponies weren't strong enough to pull them. They decided to drag the sleds to the Pole themselves.

When they finally arrived on 17 January, 1912, they saw the Norwegian flag. Downhearted, hungry and exhausted, they began to retrace their steps. But Evans was injured and died in February. Oates disappeared soon after. The three remaining men perished, too, as they sheltered from the blizzards. So close to safety, Scott wrote in his diary, "These rough notes and our dead bodies must tell the tale."

South Pole

Scott reached a record furthest south on his Antarctic journey of 1902.

## ANTARCTICA

SOUTH POLE

Beardmore glacier

Ross Ice Shelf

Bay of Whales

Ross Sea

Cape Evans

---

## AMUNDSEN REACHED THE POLE FIRST, BUT TRAGEDY OVERSHADOWED HIS ACHIEVEMENT

**1914** Heroic British explorer, Ernest Shackleton, embarks on his third Antarctic expedition.

**1915** The Endurance is trapped in pack ice. After nine months it starts to sink. Shackleton and his men take to the ice.

**April 1916** When the ice starts breaking up, they use lifeboats to struggle to Elephant Island.

**May 1916** Leaving the others behind, Shackleton and five others sail 1,125 km to South Georgia to get help.

**August 1916** The 23 desperate men on Elephant Island are finally rescued.

# 1910 Wilfred Thesiger 2005

The great Empty Quarter of Arabia is a scorching landscape of shifting sand dunes. Only Bedouin nomads have learned to survive there. When Englishman Wilfred Thesiger decided to explore the Empty Quarter in 1945, he knew he would need the help of these people or the desert would defeat him. His party started their journey at Salala, headed towards the Empty Quarter's southern edge. On the long trek Thesiger shared the hard life of his Bedouin companions, and relied on their ability to find waterholes and oases. He ended his journey deep in Oman, before returning to Salala.

On the explorer's second expedition, two years later, he braved the western Empty Quarter. From Al Mukalia in Yemen, he journeyed towards Sulayyil and the Tuwayq Mountains. Hunger, thirst, and hostile raiding parties were ever-present dangers. But still fascinated, he made a third crossing in the north, travelling east to the coast of the Persian Gulf. It wasn't long after this that oil was found in the Empty Quarter, and industry changed Thesiger's beloved desert for ever.

Persian Gulf

Saudi Arabia

Tuwayq Mountains

Liwa Wells

As Sulayyil

EMPTY QUARTER

Oman

Salala

Yemen

Al Mukalia

**N HIS BOOK *ARABIAN SANDS*, THESIGER DESCRIBED HIS ROMANTIC DESERT JOURNEYS.**

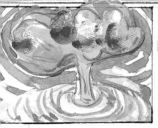

**1940s** The world enters the Atomic Age.

**1943** America pumps oil 2,080 km from Texas to Pennsylvania.

**1945** World War II in Europe ends.

**1947** Some Americans claim to see flying saucers.

Edmund Hillary

AFRICA
SAUDI ARABIA

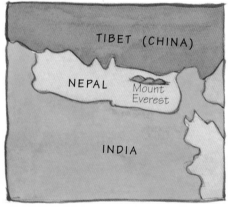

people
on the s
slopes of the
Himalayas in Nep
Although they are
renowned for their
mountaineering skills,
the Sherpas were
more often porters on
Western expeditions
than full members of the
climbing team, so Sherpa
Tenzing was unusual.
Because he was used to
mountain living, he could
cope better than the
Europeans with the lack
of oxygen at high altitude.

TIBET (CHINA)

NEPAL   Mount Everest

INDIA

Rising to an incredible 8,848 metres, Mount Everest in the Himalayas is the world's highest peak. The first people ever to climb right to the top were Sherpa Tenzing Norgay and the New Zealander Edmund Hillary. They were supported by 10 other climbers and 36 Sherpa porters. Approaching from the southwest, the team began their ascent in March 1953. They set base camp at the Khumbu Glacier, where they accustomed themselves to altitude at 6,000 metres. Beyond them, above the crevasses and ice towers of the glacier, loomed the Western Cwm (valley) and Lhotse peak. British expedition leader John Hunt and his best climbers forged ahead to the South Col, but Tenzing and Hillary chose to climb the Southeast Ridge. They camped overnight on a ledge of frozen snow. Next morning, roped together, they struggled up the South Summit and a 12-metre rock wall. Their great effort was rewarded when, at 11.30 a.m. on 29 May, 1953, they finally arrived at 'The Roof of the World' – Everest's summit.

Hillary and Tenzing planted three flags at the summit: the Nepalese and United Nations flags and a Union Jack. Then Hillary set down Hunt's crucifix and Tenzing made a Buddhist offering of biscuits to the great mountain they had just conquered.

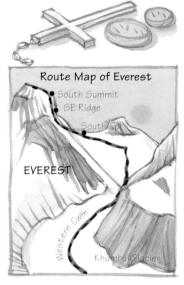
Route Map of Everest
South Summit
SE Ridge
South Col
EVEREST
Western Cwm
Khumbu Glacier

## TENZING AND HILLARY MADE FIRST ASCENT OF THE WORLD'S HIGHEST MOUNTAIN.

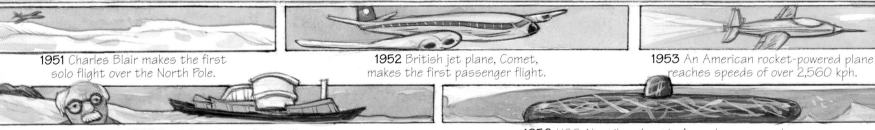

1951 Charles Blair makes the first solo flight over the North Pole.

1952 British jet plane, Comet, makes the first passenger flight.

1953 An American rocket-powered plane reaches speeds of over 2,560 kph.

1955 British engineer, Cockerell, invents the hovercraft.

1958 USS Nautilus, America's nuclear-powered submarine, passes under the North Pole.

# The Canine Cosmonauts

Laika

Bielka & Strelka

The Russians and Americans used animals to see if space technology was safe for humans, and to measure how flight affected their bodies. The Russians preferred using dogs and rodents; the Americans used rhesus monkeys and chimps.

The first living being to travel into space wasn't a person, it was a small dog. Laika – which means 'barker' in Russian – was launched in the tiny Sputnik 2 satellite on 3 November, 1957. Sealed snugly in a cylindrical cabin, she was given just enough food, drink and air for a short flight. As she orbited 1,600 kilometres above the Earth, scientists studied her heart and breathing, and observed how she was affected by weightlessness. They also measured ultraviolet and cosmic radiation outside the craft. Unfortunately, they weren't clever enough to bring Laika home. The first canine cosmonaut died in space, only a week after launch.

Strelka (Little Arrow) and Bielka (Squirrel) were luckier. They were sent into space in August 1960 with a few plants, 40 mice, and a couple of rats. After a day in orbit, they were brought back safely to Earth.

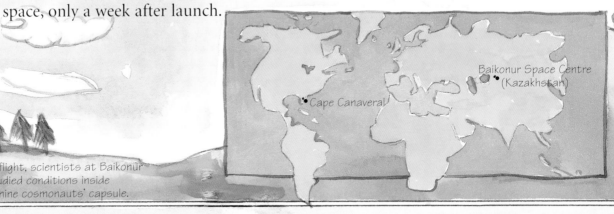

Baikonur Space Centre (Kazakhstan)

Cape Canaveral

During each space flight, scientists at Baikonur Mission Control studied conditions inside and outside the canine cosmonauts' capsule.

## DOGS, MONKEYS AND RODENTS WERE THE FIRST SPACE PIONEERS.

**1958** Gordo the monkey sinks along with his rocket.

**1959** The monkeys Able and Baker come home safely.

**1960** Sam the rhesus monkey journeys 150 km into space.

**1960** Miss Sam is used to check rocket escape systems.

**1960** Pchelka and Mushka become the third Soviet canine team.

**1961** Ham the monkey tests America's Mercury capsule.

**1961** Chernushka (Blackie) shares her capsule with mice, a guinea pig and a dummy cosmonaut.

**1961** Zvedochka (Little Star) is the last animal in space before Yuri Gagarin.

**1961** Enos the chimp experiences weightlessness and extreme forces!

# 1934 Yuri Gagarin 1968

John Glenn

Gagarin's flight took place a few years after the Soviet Union launched the world's first artificial satellite, in 1957. Sputnik 1 orbited for 92.6 minutes at heights of between 229 and 946 km above the Earth.

By the early 60s, the Russians were confident enough to move on from canines and send a human into space. On 12 April, 1961, Air Force Major Yuri Gagarin was strapped securely into his Vostok 1 satellite and soared into orbit from Kazakhstan's Baikanur space centre. In order to reach a speed of 28,000 kilometres per hour, Gagarin had to withstand huge forces of acceleration – five to ten times normal gravity. At the time, no one knew if a human could survive this, but the physical stress and prolonged weightlessness didn't seem to cause the young Russian any harm. Not needing to fly the spacecraft himself, he had time to report on what he saw – the dark sky around him, and a blue Earth below, with its seas, mountains, big cities, rivers and forests all clearly visible. Gagarin spent 89 minutes in orbit before the Vostok braking rockets fired, signalling the end of the mission. After re-entry, he parachuted safely to land, and received a hero's welcome.

Baikanur space centre

America was stung by the Soviet Union's lead in the Space Race. In February 1962, after NASA (National Aeronautics and Space Administration) was set up, they matched the Soviets by sending John Glenn on a three-orbit flight in a Mercury spacecraft.

President Kruschev of the Soviet Union showered Gagarin with honours. The young cosmonaut received the Order of Lenin, became a Hero of the Soviet Union, and also a Pilot Cosmonaut of the Soviet Union. There are even Gagarin statues.

## THE RUSSIANS STARTED A NEW ERA IN SPACE EXPLORATION.

**1963** Valentina Tereshkova is the first woman in space.

**1965** Alexei Leonov is the first man to walk in space.

**1965** America's probe Mariner IV orbits and photographs Mars.

**1967** Cosmonaut Komarov dies durin his Soyuz 1 Earth re-entry.

# 1922 Jacques Piccard

Auguste Piccard

The first submersibles were 'bathyspheres', which means 'deep spheres'. Auguste Piccard's submersible was a 'bathyscaphe' ('deep boat'). It had two parts: a floating cylinder at the top and a 14-ton steel ball hanging below. The men sat in the ball, carefully controlling their ascent and descent.

Born into a family of Swiss scientist-explorers, Jacques Piccard made his mark in deep-ocean exploration. In 1960, he and an American naval officer Donald Walsh plunged a record 10,916 metres to the lowest point on Earth, 'Challenger Deep' in the Marianas Trench. It took five hours to make their descent into the inky-black waters before their craft *Trieste* came to rest on the ocean floor. No one has ever repeated this incredible feat.

The *Trieste* was designed by Piccard's father, Auguste. As Jacques peered through its 20-centimetre-thick porthole on the ocean depths, he was amazed to see a flat fish swimming by. This tiny creature was withstanding water pressure of over a thousand times greater than at the ocean's surface! Piccard followed his achievement with another dive in 1969. This time he explored the currents in the *Ben Franklin*, which drifted all the way from Florida to east of Cape Cod.

The US Navy used Piccard's *Trieste* twice in the 1960s to search for the lost submarines *Thresher* and *Scorpion*, both of which were found. Surprisingly, *Trieste* was rarely used again for exploration.

Cape Cod
Florida
Marianas Trench

The makers of Star Trek named the captain of the *Starship Enterprise* Jean-Luc Picard, in honour of Jacques.

## PICCARD EXPLORED THE DEEPEST POINT ON EARTH IN HIS FATHER'S SUBMERSIBLE.

Vinland  Markland  Helluland

**1960** America's nuclear submarine, the *Triton*, circumnavigates the globe underwater.

**1965** Yale University says the 'Vinland Map' is no forgery. It proves the Vikings reached America in the 11th century.

**1966** A German team climbs the north face of the Eiger.

# Armstrong, Aldrin and Collins

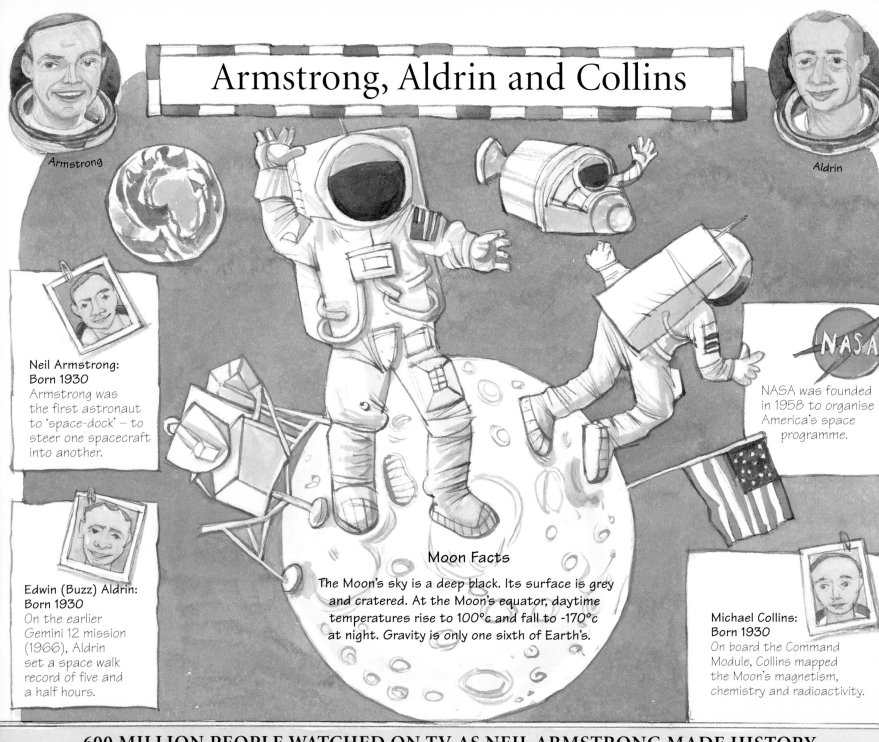

Armstrong

Aldrin

**Neil Armstrong:
Born 1930**
Armstrong was the first astronaut to 'space-dock' – to steer one spacecraft into another.

**Edwin (Buzz) Aldrin:
Born 1930**
On the earlier Gemini 12 mission (1966), Aldrin set a space walk record of five and a half hours.

NASA was founded in 1958 to organise America's space programme.

**Michael Collins:
Born 1930**
On board the Command Module, Collins mapped the Moon's magnetism, chemistry and radioactivity.

## Moon Facts

The Moon's sky is a deep black. Its surface is grey and cratered. At the Moon's equator, daytime temperatures rise to 100°c and fall to -170°c at night. Gravity is only one sixth of Earth's.

## 600 MILLION PEOPLE WATCHED ON TV AS NEIL ARMSTRONG MADE HISTORY.

The Lunar Module descends at 40 metres per second.

At 4.17 p.m., the Lunar Module lands.

The astronauts move in big, bouncing steps.

Aldrin and Armstrong plant the American flag on the Moon's desolate landscape.

Collins

Luna IX (USSR), Feb 1966

Surveyor 1 (US), May 1966

Zond 5 (USSR),1968

Lunar Orbiter (US), 1966-67

Ranger 7, 8 and 9 (US), 1964-65

Sea of Tranquillity

Ocean of Storms

## Moon Facts

America and the Soviet Union were space race rivals, and both sent space probes to the Moon. These small, unmanned spacecraft attached themselves to the Moon's surface and collected scientific data, which was studied back on Earth.

The 20th July, 1969 was the beginning of an exciting new stage in human exploration. It was the day that Neil Armstrong became the first person to set foot on the Moon. The three-man Apollo mission blasted off from Florida in America and took four days to settle into orbit. Then Michael Collins piloted the Command Module while his colleagues guided the Lunar Module, the *Eagle*, down to the Moon's surface. Their target was the smooth Sea of Tranquillity about 100 kilometres below. "The *Eagle* has landed!" said Armstrong as they touched down. Hours later he stepped on to the Moon's powdery surface, and uttered the immortal words, "That's one small step for a man, one giant leap for mankind." Armstrong and Aldrin spent about twenty-one hours on the Moon, gathering rock samples, taking photographs and doing scientific experiments. Then it was time to return to the Command Module, and begin their journey back to Earth.

### The Saturn V Rocket
Saturn V's powerful engines provided the thrust that pushed the Apollo into space from Cape Kennedy, USA on 16 July, 1969.

This is the greatest week in the history of the world since the Creation!

President Nixon

## CONNECTED BY RADIO TO EARTH, THE ASTRONAUTS REPORTED THEIR FINDINGS.

**c.600 BC** Babylonian months begin with each new moon.

**c.700 AD** The ancient Muslims inherit and develop the lunar calendar.

**1610** Galileo studies the Moon with a telescope.

**c.1870** The French writer Jules Verne imagines a Moon landing.

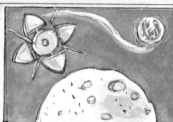

**1966** The Soviet Luna IX probe is the first to land on the Moon.

# 1914  Thor Heyerdahl  2002

Heyerdahl had an ecological worldview. He believed that eveything is inter-connected, including people who live as far apart as Peru and Easter Island.

But most experts still believe that the first people to settle on the Polynesian Islands in the Pacific came from Asia in the west.

By the 1900s, technology had made it easy for anyone to travel to far-off places, so the Norwegian explorer Heyerdahl decided to venture into the distant past instead. He studied the customs of the ancient Polynesians, and found that they had things in common with the people of South America. Experts had always believed that the first Polynesians sailed across the Pacific from Asia in the west, but Heyerdahl suggested that these settlers had made a different journey, from South America in the east. To prove that such a voyage was possible, he and five others left Peru in 1947 on a primitive balsa-wood raft called the *Kon-Tiki*. People said they would sink but, after 100 days they arrived triumphant at the Tuamotu Archipelago in Polynesia.

On a second expedition in 1970, Heyerdahl and his crew sailed *Ra II*, a papyrus boat, from Morocco to Barbados. This time they proved that the ancient Mediterranean people could have made it across the Atlantic to America. Heyerdahl's last great voyage, in another reed boat called the *Tigris*, took him from modern Iraq down the Persian Gulf to India, then across to Northeast Africa. The Arabs of the ancient past could well have made this journey.

*Ra II*

*Tigris*

*Kon-Tiki*

## HEYERDAHL PROVED THAT ANCIENT SAILORS COULD HAVE TRAVELLED HUGE DISTANCES.

**1941** Hans Haas takes the first underwater photographs.

**1941** An aircraft crosses the Atlantic in less than nine hours.

**1942** Von Braun and his team invent the powerful V2 missile in Germany.

**1943** French divers Gagnan and Cousteau invent the scuba aqualung.

# 1935 Sylvia Earle

Earle still hopes to equal Piccard and Walsh's achievement, which is to explore the deepest point on Earth – 'Challenger Deep' off the Philippines, 10,916 metres down in the Pacific.

During her long career as a deep-sea explorer, Sylvia Earle always used the latest technology. She was one of the first divers to wear modern SCUBA gear (Self-Contained Underwater Breathing Apparatus), and she later used submersibles – underwater vessels – to study marine ecosystems. In 1970, she and some other 'aquanauts' lived for 14 days in an underwater chamber. Always a pioneer, in 1979 Earle descended 385 metres to the ocean floor off Hawaii. It was the deepest ever solo-dive made without a tether line to the surface. To survive the intense water-pressure Earle had to wear an armoured diving suit. Strapped to the front of a submarine, she descended to the seabed, stepped off, planted an American flag, and explored. In the 1980s, Earle and her husband Graham Hawkes, designed some underwater robots and a one-person submersible. Aboard this *Deep Rover*, Earle made a record descent into the ocean depths.

NASA, the US Government and the Navy ran the underwater Tektite Project in 1970. The Tektite Project was America's marine version of NASA's Skylab space station. NASA also adapted Earle and Hawke's underwater technology for use in space exploration.

In over 6,000 hours of underwater exploration, Earle noted the terrible damage humans have wreaked on marine ecosystems.

Sea creatures that were named after Earle:
*Pilina Earli*, a marine plant
*Diadema Sylvie*, a sea urchin

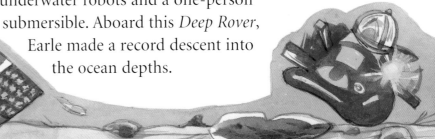

## EARLE USED MODERN TECHNOLOGY TO EXPLORE THE OCEAN DEPTHS.

**1979-82** Ranulph Fiennes leads the Transglobe Expedition, the first round-the-world land journey via both the North and South Poles.

# Final Frontiers – Ocean Depths

Pacific Ocean

Atlantic Ocean

Two final frontiers challenge 21st-century explorers: the Inner Space of the Earth's oceans, and Outer Space – the Earth's solar system. The oceans still hold many mysteries. Although most of them are about 4000-metres deep, only the top 1000 metres has been closely examined. Now governments are embarking on a new era of deep-ocean exploration, using submersibles and underwater observatories. Even so, less money is spent on developing this technology than on space flight.

The scientists who study the final ocean-frontier will be able to tell us more about life's origin on Earth, and how its marine ecosystems are best protected from human greed and carelessness. Their deep-sea discoveries will help medical research and future biotechnology industries. Our governments also hope to mine ocean minerals for industrial use and energy.

Rich coral reef habitats

Underwater mountains

Ocean currents welling up from the deep

Submarine canyons

Strange deep-ocean creatures and bacteria which need chemicals rather than sunlight to live

Erupting submarine volcanoes

Chimney-like 'smokers' – hydrothermal vents which spout hot, mineral-rich water

Deep ocean trenches – the lowest points on Earth

## WE KNOW MORE ABOUT THE MOON THAN EARTH'S DEEP OCEANS.

**1962** Jacques Cousteau and his team live on compressed air for a week in the first underwater habitat.

**1977** The Alvin submersible helps scientists discover deep hydrothermal vents and their strange ecosystems.

**2000** US President Clinton calls for a new era of Ocean Exploration.

# Final Frontiers – Space

Earth

Sun

In 2002, the US space probe 'Odyssey' discovered great oceans of ice underneath the surface of Mars. This important finding means that space scientists of the future will be able to visit the 'Red Planet' without having to carry bulky water supplies. A voyage from Earth would take about eight months, and only a perfect landing on the planet's surface would ensure the astronauts' survival. Scientist-explorers and their families could follow later, living and growing food on the planet in bio-dome habitation units. The Martian water would keep them alive, and also help them make fuel. However, the real dream of the future is a 'terraformed' Mars – a living planet just like Earth, created from vast masses of carbon dioxide, released to bring about global warming.

Pathfinder's 'Sojourner' buggy (or rover) analysed Martian rocks.

Orbiting space station

### Mars Facts

Mars has a third of the Earth's gravity, but the same length day. It is very cold now, but 4 billion years ago it had water – vital to life – and an atmosphere. This frozen water now lies a few metres below the Martian surface.

The 1996 Pathfinder probe took a remote-controlled buggy to Mars.

Astronauts are currently training in the Arctic to prepare for freezing Martian conditions. The first explorers there will have to build 'habitation units' to live in. Instant communication with Earth – something like e-mail – will also be essential. Outside, robots will gather information and create water from Mars' atmosphere.

Future Mars rovers will be manned.

Habitation units which operate as waste-free 'closed-loop' life-support systems

A re-usable rocket
Unlike Saturn V, this one can be launched more than once.

## THE QUICKEST ROUTE TO MARS IS ABOUT 160 MILLION KILOMETRES.

1964 The first close-up photos of Mars.

1971 Mars 2 (USSR) crashes on Mars.

1975-76 US Vikings 1 and 2 land on Mars.

1996 Pathfinder (US) samples rocks.

1997 Mars Global Surveyor (US) finds evidence of water.

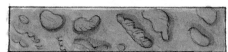
2001 Martian meteorite ALH 84001 is thought to show traces of life.

2003 UK Beagle probe planned to arrive on Mars.

2018 The first crewed return flight to Mars.

# Glossary

**Antarctic Circle** an imaginary circle going round the Earth at latitude 66° 32' S, which encloses the area around the South Pole.

**Antarctica** the large landmass (continent) around the South Pole.

**Anthropologist** a scientist who studies humans and their societies.

**Arctic Circle** an imaginary circle going round the Earth at latitude 66° 32'N, which encloses the area around the North Pole.

**Asteroid** a small planet.

**Astronaut** someone who has been trained to travel in space.

**Astronomer** a scientist who studies the universe beyond Earth, for example, the stars and planets.

**Australian Aborigines** the people who lived in Australia before explorers from Europe arrived. Their descendants still live in Australia today.

**Aztecs** the Native American people who inhabited present-day Mexico from around AD1100.

**Balsawood** the lightweight wood of a tropical tree. It is excellent for making rafts.

**Barbarians** a term used to describe people who don't belong, often enemy tribes. Barbarians are sometimes thought to be wild or warlike.

**Bedouin** a member of one of the Arab tribes who wander across the desert, and have no fixed home.

**Binary star** one of two stars that revolve around each other.

**Biodome** a dome-shaped structure that holds living and growing organisms (like plants and people) inside.

**Botanist** a scientist who studies plants.

**Bubonic plague** a deadly, highly infectious disease, caused by the bite of an infected rat flea. An early symptom of the plague was a swelling in the armpit or groin.

**Cape** a piece of highland jutting out into the sea.

**Caravel** a small, fast ship used by the Portuguese and Spanish in the 15th and 16th centuries.

**Cartographer** someone who makes maps.

**Chronometer** a very accurate timepiece or clock, used by mariners to work out their position at sea.

**Circumnavigation** sailing all the way around something – Australia, for example.

**Closed-loop life support system** a sealed unit capable of keeping living things (people, for example) alive, without any contact with the outside environment.

**Col** a low ridge that connects two mountain peaks.

**Colonization** when people set up a new community in an unknown land.

**Command Module (Columbia)** the part of the Apollo 11 spacecraft that held the control centre and living quarters.

**Compass** an instrument, usually with a magnetic needle, which tells you where north is, and so enables you to work out your exact position.

**Constellation** a fixed group of stars that make up a recognisable shape when seen from Earth.

**Cosmography** the mapping and description of the universe.

**Cosmonaut** another name for an astronaut, usually from Russia.

**Cossack** a peasant people who live in parts of Southern Russia, the Ukraine and Siberia.

**Creek** a narrow inlet.

**Crevasse** a deep crack in the thick ice of a glacier.

**Dead reckoning** a method of calculating a ship's position at sea based on the distance and direction travelled.

**Delta** a triangular area of land made up of grit, sand and gravel, dropped from a river at its mouth (the point where it meets the sea or a lake).

**Diplomat** someone who helps manage the relations between different countries or states.

**Dutch East India Company** a company of Dutch merchants who traded with the East Indies from the beginning of the 17th century.

**East Indies** the name used by European explorers of the 15th century for the islands that lie southeast of Asia, like Java, Sumatra and Borneo, together with India and the Malay Peninsula. Nowadays the East Indies usually means only the islands southeast of Asia.

**Empire** a large territory made up of many countries or states, ruled over by one powerful person or state.

**English East India Company** a company of English merchants which was set up to trade with the East Indies at the beginning of the 17th century. The company went on to manage Britain's territory in India.

**Expedition** a journey or voyage with a particular purpose.

**Flash flood** a sudden flood that is over quickly.

**Fool's gold** a shiny yellow mineral that is sometimes mistaken for real gold.

**Fossils** the remains, or imprints of prehistoric plants or animals, usually found in rocks.

**Founder** (of a ship) to fill up with water and sink.

**Frontiersmen or women** the people who lived near the North American wilderness, at the edge (frontier) of the area settled by white people.

**Geologist** a scientist who studies the history, structure and composition of the Earth, especially rocks.

**Glacier** a slow moving mass of ice.

**Great Southern Continent** a mythical landmass in the South Seas, which early explorers thought existed. The Great Southern Continent, was believed to balance with the landmasses of the Northern Hemisphere.

**Gulf** an expanse of sea that is almost enclosed by the sweep of the coast.

**Hemp** a plant from which a fibre can be extracted to make rope or canvas.

**Himalayas** a vast mountain range in South Asia. Its highest peak is Mount Everest.

**Humanitarian** having the best interests of people, or humankind, at heart.

**Humidity** the amount of moisture or dampness in the air.

**Hydro-thermal vent** an opening in the ocean floor, where very hot water flows out into the deep ocean, having being heated by hot rocks in the Earth's interior.

**Ice Age** a period when large parts of the Earth are covered with thick ice. The coldest part of the last Ice Age (the Pleistocene) ended about 15,000 years ago.

**Ice floes** sheets of floating ice.

**Indigo** blue dye made from the indigo plant. The blue colour itself is also called indigo.

**Infrared solar radiation** the sun's rays in the form of invisible light – i.e. where the light's wavelength is longer than visible red light.

**Inuit** the native people of Canada, Alaska and Greenland; sometimes known as Eskimos.

**Ivory** the hard white substance that the tusks of elephants, walruses and other animals are made from. Ivory is highly prized by some people.

**Kayak** an Inuit canoe, traditionally made of sealskin, and used for hunting at sea.

**Latitude** the distance in degrees north or south of the equator, the imaginary line which goes round the Earth at latitude 0°.

**Lodestone** an iron-rich rock which is naturally magnetic, and so can be used as a simple compass.

**Longitude** Whereas lines of latitude run east to west, and are drawn around the Earth parallel to the equator, lines of longitude are the imaginary lines that geographers have drawn around the Earth from the North to South Poles. If a point on the Earth has a longitude of 0°, it lies somewhere along the line of longitude that runs through the town of Greenwich in England. This line is known as the Greenwich Meridian.

**Lunar Module (Eagle)** the small section of the Apollo 11 spacecraft which made the first landing on the Moon in 1969.

**Magnetic Poles** the points near the extreme north and southern parts of the globe, from where the Earth's invisible magnetic field originates.

**Malaria** a disease which is caused by a parasite entering a person's bloodstream after he or she has been bitten by an infected mosquito.

**Maori** a member of the Polynesian people who have lived in New Zealand since before the arrival of European settlers.

**Marine ecosystem** a community of organisms living in an interlinked relationship with each other and their ocean environment.

**Mid-Atlantic Ridge** a (mostly) underwater volcanic ridge running north-south along the bed of the Atlantic Ocean, at the midpoint between Europe/Africa and North/South America.

**Middle East** a large area of Southwest Asia and North Africa between the Mediterranean and Pakistan, which includes the Arabian peninsula.

**Milky Way** the galaxy or belt of faint stars in our night sky, of which our Solar system is a part.

**Missionary** someone who travels to another country or place to convert the local people to their own religion.

**Moluccas** a group of islands in present-day Indonesia. The Moluccas used to be called the Spice Islands.

**Mongol** the nomadic people of East Central Asia who built a large empire in the 13th century.

**Native Americans** the native people of North, Central and South America, who were settled in America before the arrival of European explorers. Also called American Indians.

**Natural selection** the theory put forward by Charles Darwin that the animals and plants that are best suited to their environment will survive and breed more efficiently than others.

**Naturalist** an expert in natural history: the study of animals and plants in the wild.

**Navigable** describes a sea or river where it is possible for ships to sail.

**Navigator** someone who explores by sea, who is skilled in planning and sailing a course towards a destination.

**The New World** the name the Europeans gave to the newly discovered Americas (North America, Central America and South America).

**Nomad** a member of a group of people who roam from place to place.

**North Pole** the northernmost point of the Earth, around which it revolves.

**Northeast Passage** the risky sea route from the Atlantic to the Pacific Ocean that goes north of Europe and Asia, by way of the Arctic Ocean.

**Northwest Passage** the dangerous sea route from the Atlantic to the Pacific Ocean through the Arctic waters of Northern Canada.

**Oasis** a fertile place in the desert where there is water.

**Oceanographer** a scientist who studies the oceans.

**Old Spanish Trail** originally an ancient Native American trade route, the Spanish Trail became important for Mexican and white American traders between Santa Fé, New Mexico and Los Angeles in California. They carried their goods on mule trains.

**Oregon Trail** an American pioneer trail stretching from Missouri to Oregon.

**Outrigger canoe** a canoe with a log fixed to it on the outside, for stability.

**Paddle steamer** a steamboat powered by a paddle wheel.

**Papyrus** a water plant used by the ancient Egyptians to make paper.

**Peninsula** a piece of land that is almost surrounded by water. A piece of land that is completely surrounded by water is an island.

**Pioneer** an explorer or settler who is amongst the first to reach a new area – although native people may already be living there.

**Plateau**  an area of high level ground.

**Polynesian**  a member of the native people who live on three great groups of islands in the Pacific Ocean, which include New Zealand, Hawaii, the Marquesas and Samoa.

**Prehistoric**  relating to a time before history was written down.

**Quadrant**  an instrument once used in navigation and astronomy to measure the distance of stars.

**Radioactivity**  when the nucleus (centre) of a particular kind of atom – like a uranium atom – decays, and sends out invisible rays. These alpha, beta and gamma rays can pass through solid objects.

**Reef**  a ridge of rock or coral at or near the surface of the sea.

**Refraction**  the change of direction of a light when it passes at an angle into a different material.

**River rapids**  swift currents in a steep part of a riverbed.

**Santa Fé Trail**  a North American wagon trail that stretches from Independence, Missouri to Santa Fé in New Mexico.

**Satellite**  a natural object – a moon, for example – or an artificial one – like a spacecraft – that orbits (goes all the way round) the Earth or another planet.

**Sauerkraut**  pickled cabbage, popular in Germany.

**Scurvy**  a sometimes fatal disease caused by a lack of vitamin C (which is found in fruit and vegetables).

**Siberia**  a huge territory in the northeastern part of Russia.

**Smallpox**  an easily spread, very dangerous disease which causes fever and infected spots.

**The Solar system**  the planets (including Earth), moons, comets, asteroids, meteors, etc. that orbit (go round) our Sun.

**Sound**  an old English word for a sea inlet.

**Sounding**  a measurement of water depth.

**South Pole**  the most southerly point of the Earth, around which it revolves.

**South Seas**  the southern Pacific Ocean.

**Spice Islands**  the old name for the Moluccas. European explorers were keen to reach the Spice Islands to establish a profitable spice trade.

**Strait**  a narrow sea inlet.

**Submarine volcano**  a volcano rising from the ocean bed.

**Submersible**  a submarine craft that operates at very great depths, which is used in marine research, salvage and rescues, etc.

**Surveying**  making a map or plan of an area.

**Tallow**  a hard fatty substance, mostly taken from animals, which is melted down to make candles and soap.

**Terraform**  a way (in theory) to turn a lifeless planet like Mars into one that is life-rich and has a breathable atmosphere like Earth.

**Terrestrial globe**  a globe representing the Earth.

**Tomahawk**  an axe used for fighting.

**Topographical**  describes a detailed description of the physical features of an area.

**Transcontinental**  (of a railway) going across the continent.

**Treaty**  an official, signed agreement between states.

**Tributary**  a river or stream that flows into a larger river or lake.

**Tuberculosis**  a dangerous infectious disease, which usually affects the lungs.

**Typhoid**  a dangerous infectious disease of the intestines.

**Ultraviolet radiation**  invisible light radiation. Ultraviolet wavelengths are shorter than the wavelengths of violet, visible light, which makes them invisible.

**Zoology**  the scientific study of animals.

# Index

First published in Great Britain in 2004 and in the USA in 2005
by Frances Lincoln Children's Books, 4 Torriano Mews,
Torriano Avenue, London NW5 2RZ

www.franceslincoln.com

First paperback edition published in the UK in 2006 and in the USA in 2009

British Cataloguing in Publication Data available on request

ISBN-10: 1-84507-464-5
ISBN-13: 978-1-84507-464-7

Printed in China

3 5 7 9 8 6 4 2

The Publishers would like to thank Shane Winser from the Royal Geographical Society
for acting as consultant on this book.